The Discipline of Focus

Master Deep Work, Defeat Distractions, and Unlock Peak Productivity in a Distracted World

Jordan Cross

Copyright © Jordan Cross 2025 - All rights reserved.

The content contained within this book may not be reproduced, duplicated or transmitted without direct written permission from the author or the publisher.

Under no circumstances will any blame or legal responsibility be held against the publisher, or author, for any damages, reparation, or monetary loss due to the information contained within this book. Either directly or indirectly. You are responsible for your own choices, actions, and results.

Legal Notice:

This book is copyright protected. This book is only for personal use. You cannot amend, distribute, sell, use, quote or paraphrase any part, or the content within this book, without the consent of the author or publisher.

Disclaimer Notice:

Please note the information contained within this document is for educational and entertainment purposes only. All effort has been executed to present accurate, up to date, and reliable, complete information. No warranties of any kind are declared or implied. Readers acknowledge that the author is not engaging in the rendering of legal, financial, medical or professional advice. The content within this book has been derived from various sources. Please consult a licensed professional before attempting any techniques outlined in this book.

By reading this document, the reader agrees that under no circumstances is the author responsible for any losses, direct or indirect, which are incurred as a result of the use of the information contained within this document, including, but not limited to, — errors, omissions, or inaccuracies.

Contents

Introduction: The Focus Revolution Begins	v
1. The Multitasking Mirage	1
2. The Distraction Web	13
3. The Focus Playground	25
4. Brain Toys & Clarity Tricks	35
5. The Time Stretch Secret	49
6. The Deep Work Dive	62
7. The Distraction Shield	74
8. The Focus Fuel Mix	88
9. Focus in the Storm	100
10. The Focus Payoff	112
Conclusion: Your Focus Future	125
Keeping the Focus Alive	127
References	129

Introduction: The Focus Revolution Begins

Imagine a world where you finish your day energized, not exhausted—where distractions bow to your will. Picture this: It's 5 PM, and you're not a zombie staring at a screen, wondering where the hours went. You're buzzing with a quiet thrill. Your to-do list? Crushed. Your inbox? Tamed. That project you've been dodging? Done, and done well.

You're alive, sharp, ready for what's next. So, what's stopping you from living that life? Spoiler: It's not what you think. It's not time, talent, or even willpower. It's something sneakier, something we've all been tricked into ignoring.

Welcome to the focus revolution. This book is the starting point where **focus** becomes YOUR superpower. Here's the reality: That vision feels like a fantasy because most of us are drowning. Drowning in pings, pop-ups, and people who think "urgent" means "yell louder." But here's the kicker: You don't have to live that way. This book isn't about grinding harder or guzzling coffee—it's about flipping the game board and taking back what's yours. Here's how I reclaimed my superpower, and how you can too.

The Battle for Focus

By the age of 29, I had achieved what many would call success. I had financial freedom, the ability to design my own schedule, and no external constraints forcing me into a life I didn't want. But despite having all the time in the world, I found myself unable to focus. Days slipped by in a blur of scrolling, clicking, consuming—never creating.

I had spent my late twenties pulling my life back from the edge. At 28, I was at my lowest, directionless and frustrated, trapped in patterns of self-sabotage that seemed impossible to break. I rebuilt everything—my career, my habits, my discipline. But even after turning things around, I found myself falling into a different kind of trap: distraction disguised as entertainment.

I told myself I was "relaxing," but deep down, I knew better. My mornings stretched into afternoons lost in endless doom scrolling—refreshing social media feeds, consuming content at a breakneck pace, always looking for something new, something stimulating. Each night, I promised myself I'd be more productive the next day, only to wake up and repeat the cycle. I had complete control over my schedule, yet I was squandering it.

The worst part? I wasn't happy. I had everything I thought I wanted—freedom, flexibility, and time—but without focus, it all felt meaningless. I wasn't using my time in a way that made me feel fulfilled. I was numbing myself with distractions, escaping into digital noise instead of doing work that actually mattered.

The wake-up call came on a random Tuesday. I had planned to work on a passion project, something I had been excited about for months. But instead, I spent the morning scrolling through news articles, clicking on link after link, convincing myself that I was "learning." Hours disappeared. By the time I snapped out of it, I felt drained, like my brain had been hijacked. The project sat untouched. The day was wasted. Again.

That night, I sat in silence and faced the truth: My attention was fractured, my mind addicted to novelty, my ability to focus eroded by months of overstimulation. I had conditioned myself to seek easy dopamine hits instead of deep, meaningful work.

I made a decision that night. I was done letting distractions steal my life. I started experimenting—testing different techniques, eliminating digital clutter, training my mind to focus again. The results were undeniable. Within weeks, I felt sharper, more present, more in control. I finally started creating again, instead of just consuming. My work improved. My happiness returned.

This book isn't just about focus. It's about taking back your time, your mind, and your life. I know what it's like to have freedom but no direction, time, and purpose. And I know that the ability to focus—truly focus—is the key to unlocking everything you want.

Why Focus Matters Now: If you're reading this in 2025, you know the world's messier than ever. The stakes of distraction aren't just a missed deadline—they're your mental health, your creativity, your shot at success.

Studies from 2025 reveals that distraction isn't just annoying—it's a wrecking ball. Chronic task-switching spikes cortisol, the stress hormone that turns your mind to mush. A 2024 MindSync Institute report found people interrupted every 3 minutes lose 20% of their working memory by day's end. That's not just forgetting your keys—it's losing track of who you are and what you want.

Then there's creativity. You can't dream big when your brain's ping-ponging between Slack and TikTok. A 2025 InnovateLab audit revealed 68% of professionals feel their best ideas die in the brainstorm phase, swallowed by the noise of "multitasking." That novel, that business, that solution? They're suffocating under scattered attention. Focus isn't optional for creators—it's oxygen.

And success? Forget hustle. In 2025, it's about working sharper, not harder. A McKinsey study this year showed focused workers are 2.3 times more productive than their distracted peers—and happier, too. While you're chasing inbox zero, someone else is shipping a product or living a life that doesn't feel like a treadmill. Distraction isn't just costing you hours—it's stealing your edge.

Here's the twist: We've normalized this chaos. We wear "busy" like a medal and shrug when our phones buzz us into oblivion. We've bought the lie that scattered is successful, that focus is a luxury. Wrong. In 2025, the stakes are too high to keep playing that game. Your clarity, your fire, your chance at something real—they're screaming for a lifeline. That's why focus matters now. It's not about keeping up; it's about breaking free.

What's Different Here: You've probably skimmed productivity books promising the moon—eat this, schedule that, buy our app. So why's this one worth your time? Because we're not recycling the same old playbook. This isn't about inbox zero or a rigid 5 AM routine that assumes you're a robot. We're tossing the tired tropes and bringing you something fresh, quirky, and fun.

Think of this as your guide to hacking **focus** with a wink and a middle finger to the distraction machine. We're leaning on science, but not the dry kind. Did you know a 5-minute brain game can outfocus a week of willpower? Or that your desk's smell could trick your mind into deep work? We're pulling from 2025's latest—neuroplasticity, dopamine loops, flow states—but serving it with a twist. No jargon, just tools you can use today.

And we're not stopping at theory. This book's packed with oddball hacks: reverse scheduling to stretch time, playground-inspired workspaces, a "distraction shield" that makes notifications cry uncle. It's practical, but not predictable. Plus, we're not preaching perfection. No nonsense about never checking your phone or meditating for hours.

This is for real people—messy, busy, human—who want results without losing their soul. We'll meet you where you are: swamped by emails, tempted by doomscrolling, sick of feeling foggy. And we'll hand you a lifeline that's bold and doable. No fluff—just a promise to flip your focus game upside down with ideas that stick. This isn't a lecture; it's a rebellion.

How to Use This Book: So, how do you dive in? Think of this as your treasure map to focus gold. It's built for action, not just head-nodding, with 10 chapters that take you from "Why am I so scattered?" to "I'm unstoppable." Here's the roadmap:

- Start with Chapter 1—we smash the multitasking myth. If you're still juggling, you're already losing.
- Chapter 2 unravels the distraction web, showing you what's really pulling your strings.
- Chapter 3 builds your focus fortress with quirky spaces that trick your brain into working smarter.
- Chapter 4 hands you brain games to sharpen your mind in minutes, not months.
- Chapter 5 bends time with tricks that make an hour feel productive like three.
- Chapter 6 dives into deep work, unlocking your inner genius.
- Chapter 7 shields that focus from life's chaos with practical defenses.
- Chapter 8 fuels it with body hacks—food, movement, sleep—that power your brain.
- Chapter 9 masters focus under pressure, turning storms into strengths.
- Chapter 10 seals the deal: your payoff, your life, transformed.

You don't have to read front-to-back—though it's a wild ride if you do. Dip in where you're hurting. Overwhelmed by pings? Hit Chapter 7. Brain feeling mushy? Chapter 4's your jam. Each chapter's a standalone power-up, loaded with stories, stats, and weird facts to grab you, plus moves to try now. You'll see real-life wins—case studies, anecdotes—because theory's nothing without proof. And every chapter ends with a nudge to the next puzzle piece.

Don't just skim. Do the stuff. Test a hack, tweak a tip, see what clicks. Grab a notebook—jot what works, ditch what doesn't. This isn't passive; it's a toolkit. Start small—one hour of focus a day—and watch it snowball. By the end, you'll have a custom formula that fits your life, not some guru's. No pressure to nail it all—just pick a thread and pull. The revolution starts with you, one clear-headed win at a time.

You're on the brink of something big—bigger than you think. But first, we've got to flip the script on what you believe focus really is. Multitasking's been sold as your ticket to success, right? Buckle up, because Chapter 1's about to blow that lie wide open…

Chapter 1

The Multitasking Mirage

In 2024, a study showed multitasking cuts your IQ by 10 points—more than smoking weed. Yep, you read that right. Juggling tasks doesn't make you a genius; it makes you dumber than a stoner at a math quiz. So why do we still buy the hype? Why do we strut around, proud of our split screens and buzzing phones, like we're winning at life? Because we've been sold a shiny lie—one that's been crumbling under science for years. Let's rip the mask off and see what's really going on in that head of yours.

The Brain's True Nature

Your brain isn't the superhero you think it is. It's not juggling a dozen balls in the air while whistling a tune—it's more like a frazzled chef trying to cook one perfect dish. Understanding how it actually works is step one to ditching the multitasking myth and reclaiming your focus. Let's dive into the wiring, the traps, and the magic that happens when you stop splitting your attention like a cheap pizza.

. . .

Single-Task Wiring

Here's the deal: Your brain's got a one-thread limit. Multitasking? Total fiction. Neuroscience says your gray matter's a single-lane highway, not a six-lane freeway. When you try to text, email, and brainstorm all at once, you're not doing three things—you're doing one thing badly, then another, then another. It's a rapid-fire switch, not a parallel superpower. The prefrontal cortex, that fancy bit running the show, can only lock onto one task at a time. Push it harder, and it chokes.

Then there's the dopamine trap. Switching tasks feels good—those little zaps of "I've got this" trick you into thinking you're crushing it. But it's a lie. Dopamine's the brain's reward juice, and it loves novelty, not results. Every ping, every tab, every "I'll just check this" is a hit that keeps you hooked while your output tanks. It's like chasing cotton candy instead of eating a real meal—sweet, but empty.

And don't forget attention residue. Ever notice how your last task sticks around like a clingy ex? That's your brain leaving ghosts behind. A 2023 study from the University of Sussex found switching tasks leaves mental baggage—bits of the old job gumming up the new one. You're not fully here or there; you're half-assing both. It's why you blank on names mid-meeting or lose your train of thought mid-email. Your head's haunted by what you didn't finish.

But here's the good news: Neuroplasticity means focus is a muscle. Your brain can rewire itself with practice. Ditch the juggling act, and you'll train it to lock in deeper, longer, stronger. It's not fixed—you're not doomed to scatter forever. You just need to stop feeding it chaos.

Take Jake, a programmer who tripled his output by monotasking. He used to code with Slack open, music blaring, and his phone buzzing. Deadlines slipped, bugs piled up. Then he tried one thing: Two hours, one screen, one goal. No pings, no playlists. First day? He finished a feature that usually took a week. By month's end, his boss thought he'd cloned himself. Turns out, he'd just stopped screwing his brain over.

Efficiency's Silent Killer

Switching isn't just a quirk—it's a stealth assassin. Research backs this up: You lose 40% of your time every time you hop between tasks. That's not a typo. A 2024 study from MIT clocked it—flip from writing to texting, and you're burning nearly half your efficiency. Why? Because your brain's rebooting, not gliding. It's like restarting your laptop for every new app—slow, clunky, maddening.

Stress spikes come next. Cortisol, the stress hormone, floods in when you juggle. It's your body saying, "What the hell, man?" A 2025 stress lab found task-switchers had cortisol levels 30% higher than monotaskers by noon. That fog in your head? That's not fatigue—it's your brain drowning in chemical soup. No wonder you're snappy or zoned out by lunch.

Then there's the error surge. Quality craters fast when you split focus. A University of London experiment showed multitaskers made twice as many mistakes on simple math problems. Twice! Your report's sloppy, your code's buggy, your dinner's burnt—because you're not really there. You're a ghost flitting between shadows, not a master nailing the craft.

Memory takes a hit, too. Ever forget what you were doing mid-juggle? That's not you being "spacey"—it's your brain short-circuiting. Switching scrambles short-term memory, leaving you grasping for what you just read, said, or planned. It's why you reread the same email three times or blank on that meeting you swore you'd ace.

Picture Sarah, a CEO prepping a keynote. She's on a call, typing notes, and checking her watch—classic "I've got this" vibe. Then the Zoom drops, her slides crash, and she flubs the opener live. Why? She juggled her way into chaos. One task—polishing the talk—could've saved her. Instead, she bombed, and the internet ate her alive.

Flow Over Frenzy

Now, the flip side: What happens when you stop the madness? Enter the flow state—science's name for deep immersion. It's that magic zone where time melts, work clicks, and you're unstoppable. Psychologists like Mihaly Csikszentmihalyi say that flow is the peak of human performance. And guess what? You can't get there splitting hairs between tabs.

Deep work's the ticket—going beyond shallow hustle to real, meaty effort. It's not answering emails or skimming feeds; it's crafting, solving, creating. Cal Newport coined it, but it's timeless: Focus unlocks depths multitasking can't touch. You're not just busy—you're brilliant.

Productivity's got a cap, and focus hits it. Speed's a myth—rushing scatters you thinner. A 2025 productivity tracker showed monotaskers outpaced jugglers by 50% on complex tasks. Why? They're not leaking time—they're pouring it into one bucket. Einstein knew this. He didn't scribble $E=MC^2$ while tweeting. One task, pure genius. That's the edge you're after.

Meet Alex, a writer drowning in side gigs. Blogs, tweets, freelance fluff—her novel stalled for years. Then she ditched the noise. One month, one goal: 500 words a day, no distractions. She finished her draft in six weeks, landed an agent, and never looked back. Frenzy kept her small; flow set her free.

Why We're Suckered

So, your brain's not wired for multitasking—we've got that straight. But knowing it's a bust doesn't stop us from falling headfirst into the trap, does it? We're drawn to the chaos like flies to a picnic, even though it's zapping our potential. Why? Because the world's set up a slick little snare—social lures, cultural tricks, and our own quirky flaws keep us hooked. Let's unpack why we're such suckers for this productivity-draining myth, piece by piece.

Social Bait

First off, there's the busy badge. We've turned multitasking into a status flex—like a shiny pin that says, "Look at me, I'm in demand!" You've heard it: "Oh, I'm juggling a million things today!" It's a sly boast we toss around at coffee breaks or Zoom calls. Society's drilled into us that busy means important, and nothing screams "busy" like flipping between emails and chats while nodding like you've got it all under control. Problem is, it's a hollow show—lots of noise, zero depth.

Tech's in on it, too, nudging us toward madness. Apps don't just sit there—they poke you, reward you, keep you hopping. Every ping, every red dot, every "new message" alert is a tiny high-five from your phone. Social media's the ringleader—scroll a bit, tap a heart, feel the rush. It's designed to scatter you, not settle you. Tech wizards aren't guessing here; they've got brain experts tweaking the dials to make sure you're too distracted to walk away.

Then there's FOMO, the fuel that keeps this mess burning. Fear of missing out (FOMO) has you spinning like a top. What if you don't answer that text right now? What if the group chat's buzzing and you're not in on it? What if something big drops online and you're late to the party? It's a relentless tug, yanking your attention every which way. You're not locked in—you're leaping at shadows, chasing anything that flashes.

Habits seal the deal. We're wired for frenzy after years of buzzing devices and open tabs. It's second nature now—hear a beep, grab the phone; see a notification, click it fast. Your brain's been trained to crave the jump, not the stillness. Breaking that habit isn't just tough—it's a full-on rebellion against the rhythm we've danced to for too long.

Take Mia, a college sophomore whose grades took a dive from "multitasking." She'd study with Netflix rolling, phone in one hand, and group chats lighting up the other. She swore she could handle it—until midterms crashed the party. Cs and Ds piled up, her essays riddled with typos. Then she tried a two-hour focus block—no screens, just notes. Her next paper scored an A. Too late to save the semester, but a sharp lesson: Chaos doesn't make you a star.

Cultural Con

Step back, and it's not just you—the world's rigged against focus. Open offices are a prime suspect. Noise snuffs out concentration like a wet blanket on a fire. A 2025 workplace study found these setups slash productivity by 70% compared to quiet spaces—yet companies still pack us in tight. Chattering colleagues, clacking keys, that one guy who won't stop humming—it's a focus slaughterhouse. "Collaboration" they call it, but it's just a fancy word for distraction central.

The always-on lie doesn't help. Availability's been twisted into a stand-in for output, but it's a sham. Bosses expect instant replies, Slack's a leash that never quits, and "offline" might as well be a curse. We're rated by how quick we ping back, not how well we deliver. Your inbox isn't your job, but good luck convincing the work gods who think your soul's on call.

Peer pressure keeps the con alive. Trying to keep up splits your attention right down the middle. Your friend's raving about his side gig, your coworker's juggling three projects, your sister's posting her workout live. Suddenly, you're not just working—you're in a silent race, eyes darting sideways instead of digging into your own game. It's a sprint to nowhere, and you're stuck panting on the wheel.

The media ties it up with a bow, spinning multitasking as a gift. Headlines cheer "superhumans" who juggle work, family, and a blog—pure fiction. TV glorifies the exec with six screens; influencers flaunt their "hustle" like it's a medal. It's a myth polished to look like a dream, and we swallow it whole because it feels glamorous. Truth is, they're just as burned out as the rest of us.

Inner Hooks

Don't point fingers outward yet—your own mind's playing dirty, too. Boredom's a big one. Chaos beats calm when you're itching for action. Sitting still, diving deep? Feels like a slog. So you scroll, you fidget, you bounce tasks—anything to dodge the quiet. It's not laziness; it's your brain picking a quick spark over a slow burn.

Anxiety's another culprit, splintering focus like a dropped mirror. Worry's a pro at juggling—while you're working, it's muttering, "What if you flop? What if you're late? What if they hate it?" Before you know it, you're not creating—you're battling ghosts. A 2025 psych survey found anxious folks switch tasks 50% more, chasing control that slips away.

Ego's a quiet kicker. Feeling "needed" pulls you off track like a magnet. Someone pings, and boom—you're the hero dropping everything to swoop in. It's a rush that yanks you from what counts, all for a fleeting "thanks." You're not saving the day; you're dancing for applause.

Procrastination's the final veil. Busy masks fear like a pro. Piling on small stuff—emails, tweaks, "research"—lets you sidestep the big, daunting work. You're not productive; you're stalling. That project you're ducking? It's still waiting, grinning, while you shuffle papers and call it a win.

Breaking Free

Multitasking isn't just inefficient—it's a slow and silent killer of clarity, creativity, and confidence. The good news? You can break free. And when you do, you'll discover that focus isn't just about productivity; it's a skill that rewires the way you think, work, and create.

Focus as Strength

For too long, we've been conditioned to believe that multitasking is a skill—one that demonstrates competence, agility, and ambition. But the truth is, multitasking robs us of efficiency and mental clarity. When we divide our attention, we make more mistakes, waste more time, and accomplish less with greater stress. On the flip side, **monotasking**—the radical act of doing one thing at a time—transforms the way we work and think.

Imagine a surgeon performing heart surgery while checking email. A pilot landing a plane while scrolling through the news. Sounds ridiculous, right? Yet, we expect our own minds to function under similar conditions every day. When we focus on one thing at a time, we gain clarity. Thoughts sharpen, decisions become easier, and execution improves because the brain isn't overloaded. A focused mind is a precise mind, and precision leads to better results.

Most people don't realize how much time they lose to context-switching. A study by the University of California, Irvine found that when we switch tasks, it takes an average of 23 minutes and 15 seconds to return to the original level of concentration. If you switch between tasks ten times a day, that's nearly four hours lost. Over a week? Twenty hours—half a workweek gone. Over a year? An entire month of wasted time. By focusing on one thing at a time, you reclaim that time and redirect it toward mastery, deep work, or simply living with less stress.

A scattered mind is an insecure mind. When we're spread thin, we doubt ourselves because we're constantly shifting gears before finishing anything meaningful. But when we focus, we build confidence. Completing one task at a time creates a sense of accomplishment, fuels motivation, and generates momentum. The ability to focus becomes an identity—one that others respect, but more importantly, one that we respect in ourselves.

Creativity thrives on deep immersion. Writers, musicians, designers, and innovators all describe getting lost in their craft. This flow state—where time seems to disappear and ideas flow effortlessly—is only possible with sustained attention. A composer once struggled to complete his albums because he worked in a distraction-heavy environment. His output was sluggish until he made one change: he removed all distractions during composing sessions. No phone. No internet. No interruptions. His creativity flourished, and he completed an entire album in half the time it usually took. His work felt more inspired, fluid, and effortless—all because he switched from distraction to deep focus.

First Moves

Now that we know why focus matters, how do we break free from the habit of multitasking?

The first step is awareness. Catch yourself mid-juggle. Notice when you're switching between tasks—checking messages while writing an email, opening a new tab while in the middle of a project, glancing at your phone during a meeting. The moment you become aware of the pattern, pause. Ask yourself if it's necessary to switch or if it's just an impulse. The simple act of noticing is the first step toward change.

Try this: for one hour today, commit to a single task. No notifications. No tabs open in the background. No side projects running alongside your main focus. It will feel uncomfortable at first. Your brain will crave distraction, seeking the quick hit of dopamine that comes from checking a message or jumping between tasks. But by the end of the hour, you'll notice a shift—an unfamiliar yet powerful clarity.

Our brains crave reward. That's why we instinctively check our phones or jump between tasks. But we can retrain our reward system by linking pleasure to focused work instead of mindless multitasking. Gamify deep work. Set a challenge for yourself: "If I focus for 30 minutes straight, I get a 5-minute break." Celebrate the completion of meaningful work rather than the start of a dozen unfinished tasks. Replace the quick dopamine hit of checking a notification with the intrinsic satisfaction of seeing a project through to completion.

Our culture glorifies busyness, but busyness is not the same as productivity. Progress happens when we work with precision, not chaos. Shift your mindset. Stop chasing the feeling of being busy. Start prioritizing focus.

The Prize Ahead

Breaking free from multitasking isn't just about getting more done. It's about transforming how you live.

Focus doubles efficiency. The same hours produce twice the results. There's less time spent fixing mistakes, more time spent creating meaningful work, and a renewed sense of control over time.

By embracing focus, stress decreases. The mental load lightens. There's no longer the exhausting effort of juggling too many things at once, of keeping half-formed ideas in your mind, or of switching gears every few minutes. With each moment of deep concentration, the brain learns to relax into the work instead of resisting it.

A cluttered mind creates fog; a focused mind sees clearly. Deep work sharpens problem-solving skills, decision-making, and the ability to think long-term. When we focus, we begin to think in complete thoughts instead of fragmented ones.

The most important change, though, is what focus enables in the long run. History's greatest thinkers, artists, and scientists weren't multitaskers. They were deep thinkers. Focus allows us to build something meaningful. It plants the seeds of a legacy.

In the late 19th century, Santiago Ramón y Cajal faced an unsolved mystery in neuroscience: how nerve cells communicated. At the time, the prevailing belief was that the brain was a continuous, interconnected web of neurons. But something about this idea didn't sit right with him. He needed to see the truth for himself.

Determined to find answers, Cajal locked himself away in his laboratory, spending hours each day examining brain tissue under a microscope. No distractions. No interruptions. Just pure, deep focus. He meticulously sketched what he observed, drawing detailed images of neurons by hand. And then, after weeks of undisturbed work, it clicked.

He discovered that neurons were separate, individual cells that communicated across tiny gaps—what we now call synapses. His insights completely rewrote the understanding of the nervous system and won him the Nobel Prize in Physiology or Medicine in 1906.

Cajal's breakthrough wasn't a stroke of luck. It wasn't a random flash of inspiration. It was the result of deep, focused work. Had he spent his time multitasking, answering correspondence, or skimming through competing theories without concentration, he might never have uncovered what would become one of the greatest discoveries in neuroscience.

When we allow ourselves to sit with a problem—without distractions, without interruptions—our brain makes connections that would otherwise remain hidden. The modern world may be faster, but the principle remains the same: real breakthroughs come from deep focus, not scattered attention.

Now that you understand why multitasking is a trap and how to escape it, it's time to uncover the forces that are actively working against your ability to focus.

Chapter 2

The Distraction Web

Your phone vibrates. A tiny red notification dot appears. You weren't even thinking about checking your messages, but now you can't help yourself. You tap the screen. One notification turns into five minutes of scrolling. Then ten. Suddenly, twenty minutes are gone, and you barely remember what you were doing before.

This isn't an accident. Your distractions aren't random. They are designed. Every ping, every notification, every infinite scroll has been engineered to hijack your attention. And the more time you spend locked in these loops, the less control you have over your own mind.

But there's a way to break free. And the first step is understanding how deep the trap goes.

Tech's Mind Games

Technology has made life more efficient, but it has also reshaped the way we think, work, and interact. The devices that were meant to help us focus and connect now often do the opposite. Every app and platform is built with one goal: to keep you engaged for as long as possible. These aren't neutral tools; they are sophisticated systems designed to compete for your attention.

Each time you check your phone, scroll through a feed, or open a notification, your brain reinforces a habit. And the more frequently you engage, the harder it becomes to resist. Studies show that excessive digital consumption rewires the brain, reducing our ability to sustain attention and making deep focus feel unnatural. The modern mind is in a battle it never signed up for—and the battlefield is everywhere.

Algorithm Ambush

Most people believe they control their phones, but the truth is, their phones control them. Behind every social media app, news feed, and recommendation engine is an algorithm carefully programmed to hold attention for as long as possible.

- **Predictive coding**: Apps don't just respond to your actions; they anticipate them. Machine learning analyzes past behavior to predict what will keep you scrolling, clicking, and engaging.
- **Endless scrolls**: Social media feeds never seem to end. Unlike a book or an article with a clear stopping point, platforms are designed to feed you content indefinitely, making it easy to lose track of time.
- **Push alerts**: On average, people receive over 80 notifications per day. Each one interrupts focus, pulling attention away from meaningful work.
- **Reward loops**: Likes, retweets, and comments create a powerful feedback system. Every notification releases a small dopamine hit, reinforcing the habit of checking your phone repeatedly.

In 2022, software engineer and former Google employee Tristan Harris spoke publicly about how tech companies deliberately engineer apps to maximize screen time. He described how even small design choices—such as the color of notification badges—are carefully tested to exploit psychological triggers. As a design ethicist at Google, Harris had access to internal data showing that people were becoming more addicted to their devices, often without realizing it. Realizing he was complicit in the problem, he left his job to advocate for "humane technology," calling out the industry's role in fragmenting attention and reducing mental clarity. His insights have since fueled a global movement to rethink the ethics of digital engagement.

Ping Overload

The human brain wasn't designed to process constant interruptions. Every notification, buzz, or alert creates a tiny mental cost, even if you don't respond immediately. These micro-disruptions may seem insignificant, but they add up quickly.

- **The three-second derailment**: Research shows that even a brief distraction—just three seconds—is enough to cause a significant drop in performance on a task. Once interrupted, it takes 23 minutes to fully regain focus.
- **Sound triggers**: The default notification sounds on your phone aren't just functional—they are designed to be impossible to ignore. Studies have found that even the sound of a notification—without looking at the screen—can trigger stress responses in the brain.
- **Badge bait**: Those small red notification dots aren't just for convenience. Red is a psychologically stimulating color that signals urgency, making it harder to ignore messages even when they aren't important.

- **Sync chaos**: Modern technology ensures that distractions follow you everywhere. A message on your phone appears on your laptop, tablet, smartwatch, and even smart home devices. This constant synchronization makes escaping digital noise an uphill battle.

In 2019, software developer and author Cal Newport conducted an experiment on college students struggling with focus. He encouraged them to disable all non-essential notifications and limit their email and social media use to scheduled blocks. The impact was dramatic. Students who followed the recommendations reported feeling less overwhelmed, improved their ability to retain information, and even slept better. Newport's findings became a central argument in his book *Digital Minimalism*, which advocates for intentional technology use rather than passive consumption. His work has since inspired thousands to rethink their relationship with digital devices.

Dopamine Chains

The reason distractions feel irresistible isn't just about habit—it's about **neurochemistry**. Every time you check your phone, scroll through a feed, or refresh an app, your brain releases **dopamine**, the neurotransmitter associated with pleasure and reward. This creates a feedback loop that makes distractions more tempting over time.

- **The slot machine effect**: Social media operates much like a casino slot machine. Every time you refresh your feed, you don't know what you'll get—new likes? A message? A trending post? This unpredictability makes the behavior addictive, just like gambling.
- **Social validation traps**: Humans are wired to seek connection and approval. Social media platforms exploit

this by making engagement metrics highly visible, creating a cycle where people compulsively check for new likes and comments.
- **Micro-doses of dopamine**: Each small digital reward—a notification, a text message, a news update—delivers a micro-dose of dopamine. Over time, the brain starts craving these small hits, making it harder to resist distractions.
- **Tech exploits reward centers**: Tech companies employ behavioral scientists to design features that tap directly into the brain's reward system. Their goal? To make apps as habit-forming as possible.

In 2018, former Facebook executive Chamath Palihapitiya made headlines when he admitted that social media was designed to exploit human psychology. He revealed that Facebook's engagement metrics—such as likes and shares—were intentionally structured to create dopamine-driven feedback loops. Palihapitiya described how he began to feel uneasy about the impact of these systems on users' mental health, leading him to publicly denounce the very platform he helped build. His insights helped spark widespread conversations about digital addiction and the ethics of social media.

Your phone isn't going to stop buzzing. The notifications won't turn themselves off. Social media won't suddenly become less addictive. But you can change how you interact with them. We will explore these in later chapters. For now, let's dive even deeper into the rabbit hole of the distraction web.

Society's Noise

The battle for attention doesn't just happen on your phone. It happens in the world around you—on the streets, in workplaces, and in everyday conversations. Modern life is filled with distractions disguised as obligations. The pressure to stay informed, keep up, and always be "on" creates a mental fog that fractures focus.

Most people don't realize how much of their attention is hijacked by forces outside of their control. From sensationalist news cycles to crowded work environments, society normalizes distraction and even rewards it. But those who learn to navigate this noise gain a powerful advantage: the ability to direct their attention where it matters most.

Cultural Static

There's an unspoken rule in modern life: the more plugged in you are, the more valuable you seem. You're expected to know the latest news, the biggest trends, the most viral conversations. The world is constantly updating, and if you blink, you might miss something. That fear—of being uninformed, left behind, or out of the loop—keeps millions of people endlessly scrolling, reading, and reacting. But at what cost?

The never-ending flood of news and updates doesn't just keep people informed—it keeps them overwhelmed. Sensationalist headlines, political outrage, and fear-driven narratives hijack attention, making it difficult to focus on anything for long. Instead of thinking deeply about meaningful topics, the brain becomes accustomed to shallow engagement, skimming instead of absorbing, reacting instead of reflecting.

It's not just the news. Advertisers compete for mental real estate, flooding the world with content designed to steal attention. The average person sees thousands of ads every single day, each one nudging their thoughts away from personal priorities. Then there's social media, where staying "in the know" means constantly keeping up with new trends, arguments, and viral debates. It feels like participation is a requirement, as if being uninformed means being irrelevant.

But the reality is, knowing everything doesn't make you more valuable—it just makes you more distracted. Those who reclaim their mental space don't just gain clarity; they gain the ability to think for themselves.

Workplace Snares

For many, the workplace has become an arena of constant interruption. Open offices, endless meetings, and the expectation of instant communication have made focused work nearly impossible.

Open-plan workspaces, once hailed as innovative, have turned into some of the biggest productivity killers. A study found that focus drops by nearly 70% in open offices, as background chatter, movement, and visual distractions constantly pull attention away. Then there are meetings—fifteen, twenty, sometimes thirty hours per week spent in rooms (or on Zoom calls) that rarely accomplish much.

But nothing derails focus quite like email and instant messaging. The expectation to be reachable at all times means that the moment someone starts to find deep focus, a notification appears. An email, a Slack message, a quick question from a coworker—it doesn't matter what it is. The brain is yanked out of concentration, forced to switch contexts, and by the time it gets back on track, another interruption has arrived.

The modern workplace isn't designed for deep work—it's designed for responsiveness. But responsiveness doesn't create results. Those who reclaim control of their time—by limiting meetings, setting communication boundaries, and blocking out hours for uninterrupted work—don't just get more done. They get better at what they do.

The Fear of Missing Out

It doesn't stop when the workday ends. Even in personal life, attention is constantly pulled in different directions. The fear of missing out—on social events, opportunities, or experiences—can make people feel like they need to be everywhere at once.

A woman once found herself exhausted, but she didn't understand why. She was busy, yes, but wasn't everyone? Her calendar was always full—work events, dinners, weekend outings, networking meetups. She told herself it was necessary, that saying yes to everything was a way of keeping her life full and exciting. But deep down, she felt drained.

One day, she tried something different. Instead of saying yes automatically, she paused before responding to every invitation. Did she actually want to go, or did she feel like she had to? Was she attending out of excitement or obligation? Over time, her answers became clear. She started saying no to anything that didn't feel essential, and almost immediately, her life began to shift.

With fewer commitments, she finally had space to focus on things that truly mattered. Conversations became more meaningful. Her work improved. Her stress levels dropped. The people closest to her noticed that she seemed more present, more engaged. It turned out that she hadn't needed more experiences—she had needed more depth in the ones she already had.

Maybe you feel the same way as the woman in this story. And maybe you can find solutions just like she did.

Focus isn't just about cutting distractions. It's about making better choices.

Inner Chaos

Distractions aren't always external. Some of the most powerful forces pulling attention away come from within—worry, boredom, and the overwhelming weight of endless choices. The mind is constantly seeking stimulation, jumping from one thought to the next, rarely settling long enough to gain clarity. The result? A restless, scattered mental state that makes deep focus nearly impossible.

Regaining control over attention isn't just about shutting out the outside world. It's about recognizing and quieting the internal noise that keeps the brain in a state of constant fragmentation.

Worry Webs

Overthinking is one of the biggest hidden killers of focus. The brain loves to create scenarios—what-ifs about the future, replays of past conversations, imagined disasters that may never happen. The cost of these thought loops is enormous. Studies suggest that excessive worrying can reduce cognitive performance by up to 20%. When the mind is preoccupied with uncertainty, it struggles to stay present.

Most people don't realize how much time they lose to worry. They might sit down to work, but within minutes, their mind drifts—thinking about an upcoming deadline, replaying an awkward conversation from earlier in the day, or planning for problems that don't exist yet. Even when the body is still, the brain is racing, making it nearly impossible to concentrate.

One of the biggest ironies of overthinking is that it rarely solves anything. The brain convinces itself that worrying is productive, that by rehearsing every possible scenario, it's somehow preparing for the future. But in reality, overthinking creates more stress, more hesitation, and more mental fatigue—leaving less energy for actual problem-solving.

The solution isn't to suppress worry but to recognize when it's happening. The next time the mind starts spinning, pause. Ask: Is this thought helping me take action, or is it just draining my focus? If it's the latter, let it go. Imagine the thought floating on a cloud, and when you pop it, water flows out. Feel the sense of release and let it go.

Boredom Bait

In a world of constant stimulation, stillness feels unnatural. Most people don't allow themselves to be bored anymore. The moment they feel even a hint of stillness, they reach for their phone, open a new tab, or find some quick distraction to fill the gap. But in doing so, they rob themselves of the mental clarity that comes from sitting with their thoughts.

Boredom isn't the enemy of focus—it's the doorway to it. Some of the greatest creative breakthroughs have come when people allowed themselves to be still. Albert Einstein used to stare at the walls for hours, letting his mind wander. Great musicians, writers, and thinkers throughout history have used boredom as a tool, allowing their subconscious to process ideas in the background.

The problem is, modern life trains the brain to resist stillness. Social media provides endless novelty, making it easy to hop from one piece of content to another. Even when engaged in an important task, the mind craves stimulation, looking for an excuse to switch gears. This is why so many people struggle with deep work—they haven't trained their brains to sit with a single task for long enough.

The key is to reframe boredom as a signal. Instead of seeing it as something to escape, see it as a sign that the mind is clearing space for deeper thinking. Resist the urge to fill every empty moment with distraction. Let the mind wander—it might just lead somewhere valuable.

Choice Fatigue

The average person makes over 35,000 decisions every single day. Some are small—what to eat, what to wear, which email to open first. Others are larger—career moves, financial choices, long-term commitments. But every single decision carries a cost: mental energy. The more choices a person has to make, the more drained they become.

This is why some of the most productive people in the world simplify their daily decisions. Steve Jobs famously wore the same black turtleneck every day. Barack Obama limited his suit choices to navy or gray. Mark Zuckerberg wears the same type of T-shirt. These high performers understood a critical principle: the more decisions you eliminate, the more energy you have for what truly matters.

It's not just about clothing. Every unnecessary choice—what app to use, what task to start with, what notification to check—adds another layer of cognitive load. Most people don't realize how much mental energy they waste on trivial decisions. By the time they get to the important work, their willpower is already depleted.

Simplifying decision-making is one of the most powerful ways to boost focus. Create routines, set default choices, and automate anything that doesn't require deep thought. The less energy spent on small decisions, the more bandwidth remains for real progress.

A Real-Life Shift

Anna, a 34-year-old startup founder, prided herself on being hands-on in every aspect of her business. She was involved in product design, marketing strategies, hiring decisions, and even customer service. Every day was a relentless stream of emails, Slack notifications, and meetings. Even small decisions—choosing what to wear, what to eat, which emails to reply to first—felt like a burden.

By the time she sat down to do actual deep work, she was mentally exhausted. She found herself procrastinating on big-picture tasks, not because she didn't want to do them, but because her brain was too drained from the endless micro-decisions.

One evening, after another long day of feeling like she was running in circles, Anna decided to try something radical: she would simplify everything possible.

She started with her wardrobe, narrowing it down to a few interchangeable outfits to eliminate decision fatigue in the mornings. She pre-planned her meals for the week to avoid daily indecision. She blocked off specific times for emails, only checking them twice per day. She implemented a rule: if a task wasn't crucial to business growth, it was delegated or removed entirely.

Within just two weeks, something remarkable happened. She felt lighter—mentally and emotionally. Her focus sharpened, and for the first time in months, she was able to spend uninterrupted time on strategic planning. Her productivity skyrocketed, but more importantly, she felt in control again.

What Anna learned was simple: clarity doesn't come from doing more—it comes from removing the unnecessary. By eliminating trivial choices, she freed up the energy to focus on what truly mattered. What Anna did wasn't rocket science. They are all simply tiny habits and choices that you can attempt today and experiment for a few days.

Chapter 3

The Focus Playground

Most people assume that focus is purely a mental challenge—something that relies on willpower, discipline, and motivation. But what if your environment was secretly working against you?

Your workspace, your surroundings, even the colors and sounds around you have a direct impact on your ability to concentrate. A cluttered desk, harsh lighting, constant noise—each of these elements forces your brain to work harder to stay on task. On the other hand, an intentionally designed space can make focus feel effortless, pulling you into a state of deep work without struggle.

This chapter is about building an environment that naturally enhances your attention. The goal isn't to create a sterile, minimalist workspace devoid of personality but to set up your surroundings in a way that supports deep concentration instead of constantly pulling you away. The right environment doesn't just eliminate distractions—it primes your brain to stay locked in.

Space Hacks: Designing for Focus

A well-designed workspace does more than look organized—it creates the conditions for sustained focus. When your surroundings are cluttered or chaotic, your brain must work harder to filter out distractions, increasing mental fatigue. On the other hand, a space that supports deep work makes it easier to slip into a state of flow.

Designing for focus isn't about rigid rules; it's about experimenting with what works for you. The right adjustments—whether it's clearing your desk, using specific colors, or optimizing lighting—can make focus feel effortless rather than forced. Small tweaks to your environment can have a profound impact on how easily you concentrate.

The Clutter Cleanse

Clutter isn't just a visual nuisance—it's a cognitive drain. Studies show that when your surroundings are messy, your brain has to constantly process the excess information, reducing mental clarity and increasing stress. It's the reason why a clean desk often leads to a clearer mind.

Start small. Before beginning any deep work session, take five minutes to reset your workspace. Put away unnecessary papers, remove objects that aren't relevant to the task at hand, and give everything a designated place.

Another powerful strategy is the one-task, one-space rule. If you use your desk for both work and leisure—scrolling social media, eating meals, or watching videos—your brain won't associate it with focus. By dedicating a single space for deep work, you create a mental trigger that tells your brain, *this is where we concentrate.*

For some, an ultra-minimalist setup works best, while others prefer a space with personal touches like framed photos or motivational quotes. The key is **intentionality**—making sure that everything in your environment serves a purpose rather than adding to the noise.

Using Your Senses to Boost Focus

The right sensory environment can pull you into deep work faster than sheer willpower. Small changes in what you see, hear, smell, and feel can either enhance or sabotage your focus.

Color psychology plays a bigger role than most people realize. Blue tones have been shown to improve focus and productivity, while red can increase alertness in short bursts. If your space allows, incorporating blue accents—whether through a wall color, desk accessories, or even a digital wallpaper—can subtly support better concentration.

Sound is another factor. Silence isn't always ideal for deep work. For many, low-level background noise—like white noise, instrumental music, or nature sounds—helps maintain focus. If you work in a noisy environment, noise-canceling headphones can be a game-changer.

Scent can also impact attention. Peppermint and citrus scents are known to improve concentration, while lavender can promote relaxation. A simple essential oil diffuser or even a scented candle can reinforce a focused mindset.

Finally, texture and movement can provide unconscious stimulation that prevents mental drift. Fidget tools, textured desk surfaces, or even the act of flipping through a physical notebook can keep your brain engaged without breaking focus.

Choosing the Right Tools for Deep Work

Technology can be one of the biggest threats to focus—but it can also be a powerful ally if used correctly. The key is once again... **intentionality**—using tech to enhance concentration rather than fragment it.

One of the most effective focus tools is switching to analog when possible. Writing by hand has been shown to improve retention and creativity compared to typing. If you're brainstorming, planning, or journaling, a notebook might be more effective than a digital app.

For those who struggle with digital distractions, blocker apps like Freedom or Cold Turkey can help enforce boundaries by limiting access to social media or distracting websites during deep work sessions.

Lighting also plays a critical role. Cool, bright lighting can enhance alertness, making it ideal for intensive tasks, while warmer, softer lighting is better for reflection and reading. Adjustable lighting can help match the right intensity to the task at hand.

And finally, posture affects concentration more than most people realize. A standing desk, a comfortable chair, or simply changing positions throughout the day can boost energy levels and prevent focus fatigue.

Place Power

Your workspace plays a huge role in your ability to concentrate, but staying in one spot for too long can cause your brain to stagnate. Environmental shifts—whether subtle or dramatic—can refresh your mind and reignite your ability to focus. Some of the best deep thinkers, from writers to scientists, have long known the power of changing their setting to spark creativity and productivity.

· · ·

The Power of Changing Locations

Routine is powerful, but too much sameness can lead to mental stagnation. The brain craves novelty, and shifting work locations can trick it into staying engaged longer. This is why many people find they can work productively in a café or library—new surroundings activate alertness while reducing the monotony that can lead to distraction.

Cafés, in particular, provide the perfect balance of background noise and structure. Research suggests that moderate noise levels, around 50-70 dB, can enhance concentration by keeping the mind engaged but not overwhelmed. The ambient hum of a coffee shop—people talking, the soft clatter of cups—creates a background rhythm that can boost creative thinking.

One software engineer spent years working in the same home office, convinced it was the optimal environment for productivity. Yet, despite long hours, his focus was slipping. Deadlines felt heavier, ideas weren't flowing, and work started taking twice as long. Frustrated, he decided to make a change. He began alternating between a quiet café and a local coworking space. At first, it felt unfamiliar, but within days, he noticed a difference—his concentration improved, and the projects that once dragged on suddenly moved faster. The simple act of changing locations had reset his ability to focus.

Switching locations every few days can also keep focus fresh. If you always work at the same desk, your brain starts to associate that spot with a specific mental state, which can sometimes lead to stagnation. Rotating between a home office, a library, a coworking space, or even different rooms in your house can keep your environment stimulating without being distracting.

. . .

Nature Boost: How the Outdoors Supercharges Your Mind

Spending time in nature isn't just a feel-good luxury—it's a scientifically proven way to restore focus. Studies have found that being in green spaces can increase attention span by 20%, reduce stress, and improve cognitive function.

A researcher at Stanford University conducted a study comparing two groups of people—one that took a 50-minute walk through a tree-lined park and another that walked through a busy urban environment. The results were striking. The group that spent time in nature showed significantly improved working memory and focus, while the city walkers experienced no change.

Even small doses of nature can have a dramatic impact. Taking a 10-minute walk outside can reset focus and boost creativity. If stepping outdoors isn't an option, surrounding yourself with natural elements—like indoor plants or images of landscapes—can also help. Some research suggests that looking at fractal patterns found in trees and leaves has a calming effect on the brain, making it easier to sustain deep work.

Fine-Tuning Your Surroundings for Maximum Focus

Even if you can't switch locations or step outside, there are ways to tweak your immediate environment to support better concentration.

One of the simplest adjustments? **Sound control.** Complete silence isn't always ideal for focus—many people find that soft, steady background noise can actually help maintain attention. The sound of rain, distant chatter, or instrumental music can create a consistent auditory backdrop that drowns out disruptive noise without becoming distracting itself. What works best for me to delve into deep work is "white noise with thunderstorms". You should be able to find all kinds of white noise on YouTube. I like to stick to this one and it has served me really well.

For tasks that require intense focus, lyrics can be a problem—spoken words compete with cognitive processing. Switching to instrumental music or ambient sounds can provide stimulation without interfering with deep work. Some people even find that listening to the same song or playlist on repeat helps reinforce a deep focus state, as the brain learns to associate the sound with work mode.

Temperature also plays a role. The brain operates best in a room that's around 72°F (22°C)—too warm, and fatigue sets in; too cold, and the body's discomfort distracts from the task at hand. Adjusting lighting can also make a difference—natural light is ideal, but if that's not possible, warmer lights can help signal relaxation, while cooler, brighter tones can promote alertness.

Optimizing where you work doesn't require a drastic lifestyle change. Small shifts—changing locations, incorporating natural elements, or fine-tuning the sensory details of your workspace—can dramatically improve your ability to focus. The key is to experiment and find what works best for you.

Some environments are naturally more suited for deep work than others, but ultimately, focus isn't about rigid rules—it's about creating conditions where your mind can thrive.

Fun Factor

Focus doesn't have to feel like a rigid discipline—it can be fun. Many people assume that deep work requires an intense, almost joyless state of mind, but research shows that engaging the brain in playful ways can actually enhance concentration, boost creativity, and reduce stress.

A workspace that sparks curiosity and excitement encourages the brain to stay engaged longer. Adding small elements of novelty—whether through quirky office supplies, mood-enhancing tricks, or experimental shifts in how and where you work—can help keep focus fresh and sustainable.

Quirky Gear

Sometimes, all it takes to reignite focus is a slight shift in the tools you use. Novelty captures attention, making even the most mundane tasks feel new again. Writers, artists, and designers have long known this trick—switching between mediums or using unconventional tools can break monotony and encourage deep work.

Retro tech can have a similar effect. Some writers prefer working on typewriters to remove digital distractions. Others find that using a specific pen or notebook helps signal "focus mode" to the brain. Even simple tricks—like color-coding tasks or using a fun, oversized notepad—can make work feel more engaging.

The key is to experiment. Something as small as a uniquely shaped pen or a mechanical keyboard with satisfying key clicks can transform focus by making the act of working more enjoyable.

Setting the Right Emotional Tone for Focus

Your workspace isn't just about function—it's about feeling. The brain works best when it's in a positive state, so small mood-boosting tweaks can dramatically impact productivity.

Humor, for example, has been shown to improve cognitive flexibility and problem-solving. Taking a short break to laugh—whether it's watching a funny clip, reading a comic, or chatting with a colleague—can reset focus and make challenging tasks feel less overwhelming.

In 2012, Google conducted an internal experiment at its Zurich office to study how environment impacts focus and morale. Employees were encouraged to personalize their workspaces, with some adding playful elements like posters, joke boards, or quirky desk decorations. One marketing analyst, initially skeptical, placed a small toy figurine on his desk—a reminder not to take work too seriously. Over time, he noticed a surprising shift. The visual cue became a small but effective mental reset, helping him stay focused without succumbing to stress. This experiment reinforced Google's approach to designing workspaces that blend professionalism with a touch of playfulness, proving that even minor mood enhancers can have an impact.

Lighting is another often-overlooked factor. Bright, natural light boosts energy, while dimmer, warmer light can encourage a more relaxed focus state. If you find yourself dragging in the afternoon, adjusting the lighting—whether by opening a window, switching to a daylight bulb, or adding a desk lamp—can help reset your energy.

Experiment Lab: Finding What Works for You

Focus isn't one-size-fits-all. The best way to optimize your ability to concentrate is through trial and error—testing different environments, tools, and techniques to discover what works best for your brain.

Tracking what works can be just as important as testing. If a specific setup leads to a highly productive day, take note—what was different? Was it the location? The music? The time of day? By keeping a simple focus journal or making mental notes of what conditions lead to deep work, you can intentionally recreate those conditions.

Making focus enjoyable is hugely about designing an environment where concentration feels effortless. Small tweaks—whether it's a fun tool, a mood booster, or an experiment with different workspaces—

can turn focus from a struggle into something exciting that you look forward to.

Chapter 4

Brain Toys & Clarity Tricks

Focus isn't just about willpower—it's about training your brain to sustain attention enjoyably. Just like physical exercise strengthens muscles, mental exercises can improve concentration, memory, and cognitive flexibility. The right mental workouts can make focus feel automatic rather than a constant battle.

Scientific studies show that certain games and exercises can enhance brain function, sharpening attention and increasing processing speed. These aren't just theoretical concepts—elite performers, from athletes to CEOs, use cognitive training to maintain peak mental performance. By integrating brain-stimulating activities into your daily routine, you can boost your ability to concentrate while making the process enjoyable.

Mind Gym

Focus isn't something you either have or don't—it's a skill that can be trained and refined. Attention-training games have been used in everything from military pilot training to ADHD therapy, helping individuals improve their ability to sustain focus under pressure.

One of the most well-known exercises is the Stroop Test. This simple yet powerful task requires you to name the color of a word rather than reading the word itself (for example, the word "RED" written in blue ink). The test forces the brain to override automatic responses, sharpening cognitive control. Studies have shown that regularly practicing the Stroop Test can improve selective attention, making it easier to resist distractions.

Another effective tool is the "Spot the Difference" challenge. This classic game requires careful visual scanning to detect subtle differences between two nearly identical images. It enhances attention to detail, a critical skill for anyone who needs to catch errors quickly or stay engaged in complex tasks.

Even simple mental math exercises—like counting backward by sevens or performing quick calculations—can activate the prefrontal cortex, waking up the brain and priming it for deep work. Many high-performers start their mornings with such exercises to kickstart mental clarity before diving into their work.

The key to these brain-training techniques is consistency. Just five minutes of targeted cognitive training per day can lead to noticeable improvements in focus and information processing speed over time.

Memory Jumps: Strengthening the Mind's Storage System

Memory and focus are closely connected. A scattered mind struggles to retain information, while a well-trained memory allows for deeper engagement and faster recall. Many of the world's most successful individuals use memory techniques to streamline their thinking and decision-making.

One effective method is the Grid Recall exercise. In this activity, you briefly study a grid of random numbers or symbols, then attempt to reproduce it from memory. This strengthens working memory—the brain's ability to hold and manipulate information in real time.

Another simple but powerful technique is the Word Chain game, where you build a sequence of related words in your mind (for example, "apple → banana → orange → fruit"). This strengthens associative memory, making it easier to recall information quickly.

A similar approach can be applied to numbers. Many memory champions practice a technique called the Number Run, where they memorize and recall long strings of numbers. While this may seem unnecessary for everyday life, it trains the brain to hold more information at once, improving overall cognitive endurance.

These techniques are not just for fun—they are practical tools for anyone who needs to absorb large amounts of information quickly. Whether you're a student preparing for an exam, a professional managing multiple projects, or simply someone looking to sharpen their thinking, memory training can make a significant difference.

In 2018, a university study found that students who spent just 10 minutes per day practicing memory-based games performed significantly better on tests requiring sustained focus and recall. One student, struggling with exam performance due to distractions, implemented a simple daily memory routine involving number recall and word associations. The result? Sharper focus during study sessions, faster retention of key concepts, and ultimately, higher test scores.

Puzzle Pops: Rewiring the Brain Through Play

The brain loves novelty, and puzzles provide the perfect combination of challenge and reward. Solving logic puzzles, riddles, or mazes isn't just an entertaining pastime—it builds cognitive endurance, enhances problem-solving skills, and strengthens neural connections.

Sudoku, for example, has been shown to improve logical reasoning and pattern recognition. Studies suggest that regularly engaging in Sudoku or similar logic-based games can increase mental agility and reduce cognitive decline.

Riddles and lateral thinking puzzles work in a different way, forcing the brain to break free from rigid thought patterns and consider creative solutions. Many high-achieving entrepreneurs and inventors credit their ability to "think outside the box" to a habit of engaging in brain teasers and abstract problem-solving exercises.

Even classic activities like mazes can be surprisingly beneficial. The process of navigating a maze strengthens spatial awareness, patience, and persistence—all of which translate into better focus and problem-solving ability in real life.

One real-life example comes from a retiree who had always struggled with attention lapses. At age 65, he began playing chess and Sudoku daily, treating them as a mental workout. Within a few months, he noticed an unexpected benefit—his ability to stay focused on conversations improved, reading felt more engaging, and he no longer felt as mentally "foggy" as before. The lesson? It's never too late to train your brain for better focus.

Brain-training techniques aren't about working harder—they're about working smarter. By integrating focus-building games, memory-enhancing exercises, and puzzle-solving into your routine, you create an environment where attention naturally sharpens. The best part? It doesn't feel like work. These methods transform focus into something engaging, making it easier to sustain deep concentration without feeling drained.

Quick Calm

Focus isn't just about mental discipline—it's also about managing stress and staying centered under pressure. No matter how well you optimize your environment or sharpen your attention, distractions will still arise. Unexpected interruptions, looming deadlines, and internal worries can derail even the most disciplined mind.

The ability to quickly reset—whether through controlled breathing, sensory cues, or mental visualization—can mean the difference between a scattered, anxious state and a sharp, productive one. These techniques are used by emergency responders, pilots, elite athletes, and high-pressure professionals to maintain clarity when every second counts.

Mastering the ability to reset your focus on demand will transform the way you work, think, and react under pressure. Whether it's through breath control, sensory grounding, or mental imagery, these techniques will help you regain clarity in seconds—without needing to step away or take an extended break.

Breath Snaps: Resetting the Mind in a Single Inhale

Breathing is one of the fastest ways to regulate focus. Under stress, breathing becomes shallow and rapid, sending signals to the brain that something is wrong. But by controlling breath, you can override that stress response—slowing heart rate, reducing cortisol, and restoring mental clarity.

One of the most effective methods is the **4-7-8 breathing technique**, a widely practiced method used by medical professionals, military personnel, and elite athletes to regain composure in high-pressure moments. The technique involves inhaling for four seconds, holding the breath for seven seconds, and exhaling slowly for eight seconds. The slow, controlled release of air forces the body into relaxation mode, preventing stress from hijacking focus.

Another technique, **box breathing**, is a favorite among Navy SEALs. This method involves inhaling for four seconds, holding the breath for four seconds, exhaling for four seconds, and then pausing for four seconds before repeating the cycle. The structured rhythm of this breathing technique stabilizes the nervous system, enhances oxygen flow to the brain, and creates an immediate sense of control—making it particularly effective in chaotic environments.

Breathing techniques are what helped me to focus and write this very book that you're reading right now. Feeling lethargic after lunch? 4 sets of box breathing helped me to refocus and lock in. An ancient wisdom holds true. The only thing that stays with us from the day we are born to the day we die is our breath. Learning how to better utilise creative ways of breathing for assisting us will be a game changer when you compound the effects in years, and then decades.

The Science of Breathing and Focus

Research has shown that controlled breathing can shift brain function almost instantly. A study published in *Psychophysiology* found that slow, deep breathing improves cognitive performance and reaction time, while a 2020 study from *Frontiers in Human Neuroscience* showed that structured breathing exercises enhance attention control and working memory.

One field where this technique has been put to the test is emergency medicine. During the COVID-19 pandemic, nurses in Wuhan, China, faced overwhelming pressure, leading to high stress and poor sleep quality. A study involving 151 frontline nurses found that those who practiced diaphragmatic breathing relaxation training (DBRT) experienced significantly lower anxiety levels and improved focus. For professionals in high-intensity environments, mastering breathing techniques isn't just about relaxation—it's about maintaining the ability to think critically in life-or-death situations.

These breathing techniques take less than a minute to practice, yet they create a profound shift in focus, allowing for smoother transitions between tasks and deeper engagement in the present moment.

Using Sensory Cues to Lock Into Focus

In moments of distraction, physical touch, sound, or sight can act as anchors, pulling attention back to the present. These simple but powerful cues ground the mind, preventing it from spiraling into overwhelm or mental drift.

One effective technique is the touch cue—a small, intentional movement that signals the brain to refocus. This could be as simple as rubbing hands together, gripping a desk edge, or pressing fingertips to the temples. These actions serve as a reset button, reminding the mind to stay engaged.

Sound can also serve as a powerful focus anchor. A ticking clock, the hum of a fan, or even a single deep clap can snap attention back. Many professionals use subtle sound cues—such as the chime of a mindfulness app or the quiet click of a metronome—to stay centered during deep work.

A Pilot's Pre-Flight Ritual

Pilots, responsible for operating complex machinery under extreme conditions, rely on mental anchoring techniques to ensure unwavering focus. Captain Sully Sullenberger, the pilot who safely landed US Airways Flight 1549 on the Hudson River in 2009, attributed much of his ability to remain calm and focused to well-rehearsed pre-flight rituals.

Before stepping into the cockpit, experienced pilots develop physical routines—adjusting their headset the same way each time, pressing their hands against the dashboard, or performing a brief breathing exercise. These habits condition the mind to enter a state of deep focus on command.

When distractions threaten to derail focus, anchor points act as instant resets—short-circuiting mental drift and reinforcing attention in a matter of seconds.

Vision Cues

The mind responds powerfully to images. What you visualize, you internalize. Athletes, performers, and high achievers often use mental imagery to reinforce focus, setting the stage for success before a single action is taken.

One of the simplest vision cues is the **goal flash**—a quick mental snapshot of what success looks like. Before starting a task, closing your eyes and picturing the completed outcome can lock in motivation and prevent distractions from taking hold.

Another technique is the **mind movie**, in which you mentally walk through a task before doing it. This method has been used by Olympic athletes, who visualize entire routines before stepping onto the field. Studies have shown that the brain fires the same neurons during visualization as it does during actual performance, making it a highly effective tool for sharpening focus.

An Athlete's Gold Medal Vision

Visualization has been used by some of the world's top athletes to achieve peak performance. Michael Phelps, the most decorated Olympian in history, practiced mental imagery before every race. Each night before a competition, he would close his eyes and visualize every detail of his swim—the feel of the water, the turns, the stroke technique, the finish. He repeated this mental rehearsal so often that by race day, it felt like he had already won.

A 2012 study on sports psychology found that elite sprinters who incorporated visualization techniques into their training significantly improved their reaction times and overall performance. The reason? The brain processes visualized movements almost identically to physical ones, strengthening neural pathways for optimal execution.

A simpler version of this practice involves using **color cues**—imagining a color associated with clarity, like blue or white, to trigger a mental shift into focus mode. Some professionals even keep a small object or image in their workspace as a physical reminder of their goals, reinforcing mental engagement.

When executed correctly, vision cues transform focus into something tangible, allowing the brain to lock onto a clear objective rather than getting lost in distractions.

Harnessing Instant Focus Tools

Quick resets aren't just emergency measures—they are built-in tools for maintaining sharp attention throughout the day. Whether through breath control, physical anchors, or mental imagery, these techniques offer a fast and effective way to regain clarity in seconds.

The key is **consistency**. Practicing these techniques daily, even when distractions aren't overwhelming, conditions the brain to return to focus on demand. Over time, these tools become second nature, allowing for effortless concentration, even in high-pressure situations.

By integrating **breath snaps**, **anchor points**, and **vision cues** into daily routines, you can build a focus muscle that doesn't falter under stress. The ability to stay composed, reset quickly, and engage deeply is what separates those who merely get through the day from those who master their attention and perform at their peak.

Thought Twists

Distraction isn't always about external noise or digital temptations. Sometimes, the biggest roadblock to deep focus is the way we think about tasks themselves. The mind craves engagement, novelty, and progress. Without these, even the most important work can feel like a chore, leading to procrastination, frustration, and mental fatigue.

The good news? You can trick your brain into loving focus by reshaping the way you approach work, redefining rewards, and using curiosity as a powerful motivator. The secret to deep, sustained concentration isn't forcing yourself to work harder—it's making focus naturally rewarding.

Reframing Tasks

Some tasks feel overwhelming because they appear too large, tedious, or draining. But what if the problem isn't the task itself, but how we perceive it? The brain thrives on structure, progress, and small wins. When a task feels vague or endless, resistance builds. The solution lies in breaking work into clearly defined steps.

A study by the University of Michigan found that participants who divided their workload into smaller segments experienced significantly lower stress and higher motivation than those who viewed work as one massive undertaking. The reason? Each completed step triggers a dopamine release, reinforcing focus and making momentum easier to maintain.

Author Anthony Trollope, one of the most prolific writers of the 19th century, understood this instinctively. Instead of setting a vague goal like "write a book," he broke his work into strict 15-minute writing targets. His disciplined approach allowed him to complete 47 novels while writing just three hours a day. By focusing on bite-sized progress rather than the intimidating whole, he made deep work feel manageable rather than overwhelming.

Video games are addictive because they provide immediate feedback, structured challenges, and visible progress. Applying the same mechanics to work can transform even the dullest tasks. Setting personal challenges—such as racing against a timer, tracking completed sections, or using a checklist—makes deep focus feel like a rewarding pursuit rather than a chore.

Ernest Hemingway, known for his disciplined writing habits, had a simple strategy to maintain momentum. He intentionally stopped writing mid-sentence at the height of inspiration, ensuring that when he returned the next day, he could pick up with an easy win. The brain, craving completion, naturally re-engages with unfinished work. By stacking small victories, motivation builds effortlessly.

Training the Brain to Crave Focus

Modern distractions—social media notifications, emails, and digital alerts—hijack the brain's reward system by offering instant, effortless gratification. The more these quick hits of dopamine are reinforced, the harder it becomes to sustain attention on slower, deeper work.

Breaking this cycle doesn't require more discipline; it requires retraining dopamine. The brain doesn't distinguish between productive and unproductive rewards—it simply craves the fastest hit. Shifting rewards from distractions to deep work completion rewires the brain to associate effort with pleasure rather than avoidance.

A bakery owner struggling with phone addiction used this principle to regain focus. She had developed a habit of checking notifications every few minutes, disrupting her workflow. To retrain her attention, she implemented a simple rule: she could only check her phone after finishing a full batch of baking. Initially, it was difficult—her brain craved the instant dopamine rush of checking messages. But within weeks, the pattern shifted. Her focus deepened, her work felt more satisfying, and the urge to constantly check her phone faded.

Psychologist B.F. Skinner's research on behavior reinforcement found that delayed rewards create stronger habits than immediate gratification. Small self-imposed rules—like taking a break only after a focused session or rewarding deep work with a satisfying activity—can make productivity feel just as rewarding as digital distractions.

Self-recognition is another powerful reinforcement tool. Studies from Stanford University show that self-praise activates the same reward centers as external validation. Simply acknowledging progress with a mental note—"That was a good session"—creates a neurological feedback loop that strengthens focus.

For me, food works really well. I love eating and nothing is more rewarding than a good hot meal after a 3 hour focus block in a cold room. Once again, find your own reward system! You are uniquely you and what is rewarding to you could be a disappointment for others.

Harnessing Curiosity

People naturally focus on what interests them. When a task feels dull or meaningless, the brain resists, craving more stimulating distractions. But when curiosity is engaged, attention becomes effortless.

A simple way to activate curiosity is through reframing tasks as questions. Instead of thinking, "I have to write this report," ask, "How can I make this the most engaging report my team has ever read?" The mind, wired to solve puzzles, shifts from avoidance to engagement.

A 12-year-old student, Shubham Banerjee, used this approach in 2015 when he became fascinated by a question: "How can I build a better Braille printer for the blind?" What started as a school project turned into an obsession. He spent months researching, experimenting, and refining his design, eventually building a fully functional Braille printer out of LEGO bricks. His work gained attention from Intel and led to the launch of his own company before he was even a teenager. Curiosity wasn't just a motivator—it became the driving force behind his deep focus.

Another strategy is connecting tasks to a greater purpose. In a 2019 MIT study, workers who linked daily tasks to personal meaning—such as how their work contributed to a larger goal—maintained significantly higher attention spans than those who didn't. When focus feels like a struggle, asking "Why does this matter?" or "How does this connect to something bigger?" can provide a renewed sense of engagement.

High achievers across fields—from Olympic athletes to business leaders—use visualization techniques to reinforce focus. Before a race, sprinters often mentally rehearse every step, picturing the exact moment they'll cross the finish line. Neuroscience shows that this kind of mental practice activates the same neural pathways as real performance, strengthening focus and execution. A simple version of this method is the goal flash as previously mentioned—before beginning a task, briefly visualizing the completed result. The mind locks onto the desired outcome, making distractions less appealing.

. . .

Rewiring Focus for Good

Mastering focus isn't about forcing yourself to concentrate—it's about making deep work more rewarding than distraction. By breaking tasks into manageable steps, shifting dopamine triggers, and using curiosity to drive attention, focus becomes a natural and effortless habit.

This approach doesn't require extreme willpower. It simply requires small mental shifts that turn focus into an engaging, self-reinforcing cycle. When structured correctly, deep work stops feeling like a battle and starts feeling like flow.

Now that the mind is primed for deep concentration, the next step is mastering the one resource no one can reclaim—time itself.

Chapter 5

The Time Stretch Secret

Time is the great equalizer—everyone gets the same 24 hours in a day. Yet, some people achieve more in those hours while others constantly feel behind, overwhelmed, and exhausted.

The secret to making one hour feel productive like three isn't about working harder or stretching yourself thinner. It's about harnessing natural productivity rhythms, taking intentional breaks, and aligning tasks with energy peaks. When mastered, time expands, work flows effortlessly, and deep focus becomes second nature.

Cycle Control

Most people assume that focus is a matter of willpower—that if they just push harder, they'll be able to sustain long hours of productivity. But science tells a different story. The brain works in cycles, not in a straight line.

Throughout the day, cognitive energy rises and falls in **ultradian rhythms**, which last about 90 minutes. This means focus naturally peaks and then dips. Trying to push through these low-energy phases is counterproductive—it leads to burnout, mental fog, and declining performance. The key is to work in sync with these cycles, leveraging peak moments for deep work and using natural dips for strategic recovery.

A study from Florida State University examined top performers—musicians, athletes, and chess players. The highest achievers didn't work the longest hours. They worked in highly structured **90-minute focus sessions**, followed by intentional breaks. This method allowed them to sustain high levels of performance without exhaustion.

David McWilliams, a graphic designer under tight deadlines, discovered this firsthand. He had a habit of working in long, uninterrupted stretches, often hitting a wall of frustration and creative block. On a colleague's advice, he experimented with a **90-minute deep work, 20-minute rest** routine. Instead of draining himself trying to power through, he worked in short, intense bursts, then fully disconnected during his breaks. The impact was immediate—his creativity surged, energy remained steady, and he met deadlines without the usual stress and mental fatigue.

The key to making this work is **deliberate transitions**. Before beginning a session, take five minutes to prepare—clear the workspace, set an intention, and remove distractions. At the end of the cycle, step away completely—stretch, take a short walk, or practice a simple breathing exercise. These moments of reset are not wasted time; they are what allow the next cycle of focus to be just as powerful.

Why Stopping Makes You More Productive

It's a myth that working longer means getting more done. In reality, the longer you work without stopping, the less effective you become.

Focus depletes over time, and without proper recovery, productivity takes a nosedive.

A 2019 study in *Nature* found that brief, intentional breaks increase cognitive performance. Participants who took structured breaks performed significantly better on problem-solving tasks compared to those who worked continuously. This happens because breaks prevent cognitive fatigue and restore mental sharpness.

But not all breaks are effective. Checking social media for five minutes won't restore focus—it will just introduce new distractions. The best breaks involve movement, fresh air, or sensory resets.

A high school teacher struggling with the afternoon slump tested this principle. Instead of reaching for caffeine, she made a small change—at 2 PM every day, she took a 15-minute walk outside. No phone. No emails. Just movement and fresh air. The impact was immediate. Instead of crashing, she found herself returning to her work with more clarity and energy.

Another overlooked factor is nutrition. Certain foods—especially refined sugars and processed carbs—cause sharp energy crashes. Instead of reaching for sweets or coffee, a better alternative is healthy fats and proteins, like almonds, eggs, or dark chocolate. These keep blood sugar stable and prevent mid-day brain fog.

Sometimes, the most powerful reset is stillness. Five minutes of deep breathing or simply looking out a window can clear mental clutter. The absence of stimulation allows the brain to consolidate information, recharge, and return sharper.

Task Timing: Aligning Work With Energy Peaks

Not all hours of the day are equal when it comes to focus. Some hours are primed for deep concentration, while others are better suited for lighter, less demanding work. The key to maximizing time isn't just about how you work—it's about when you work.

Cognitive psychologist Nathaniel Kleitman, a pioneer in sleep and performance research, found that people experience two primary peaks of alertness each day—one in the morning and one in the late afternoon. Understanding these natural highs and lows can help structure a workday for maximum efficiency.

A musician preparing for an upcoming concert noticed this pattern in his own practice. He struggled with early morning rehearsals but found his best sessions happened in the late afternoon. Instead of forcing himself into a rigid schedule, he adapted—reserving the most challenging work for when his mind was naturally at its sharpest.

For most people, the first three hours after waking are the most cognitively powerful. This is the ideal window for deep work—writing, problem-solving, creative brainstorming. As energy fades, tasks should become easier—meetings, emails, and administrative work fit best in the lower-energy periods of the day.

A simple way to structure work is by matching tasks to energy levels:

- **High-energy periods** (morning, early afternoon): Creative work, problem-solving, deep learning.
- **Moderate-energy periods** (midday): Meetings, discussions, collaborative work.
- **Low-energy periods** (late afternoon, evening): Emails, administrative tasks, routine work.

Another strategy is time-fitting tasks to attention spans. Large projects with high cognitive demands need longer, uninterrupted focus blocks. Meanwhile, smaller, less demanding tasks—quick emails, minor edits, short calls—can be slotted into shorter windows when energy dips.

By structuring the day around natural energy flows, time stretches effortlessly. The same work that once felt overwhelming becomes smoother, faster, and more effective.

Expanding Time Through Smarter Work

The secret to making time work for you isn't about squeezing in more tasks—it's about structuring focus in a way that feels effortless. Working in cycles, taking structured breaks, and aligning tasks with energy levels allow for maximum output with minimum exhaustion.

This isn't about pushing harder or doing more—it's about doing the right things at the right times. When time is structured well, work stops feeling like a battle and starts flowing like a natural rhythm.

Backwards Clock

Most people approach time from the present forward—starting with what needs to be done right now and working toward a deadline. But the most effective way to take control of time isn't to start at the beginning—it's to start at the end.

By flipping the way planning is done—working backward from the desired outcome—it becomes easier to eliminate wasted effort, avoid false urgency, and ensure that every step contributes to meaningful progress. This approach isn't just about managing time; it's about designing it so that every hour is used with purpose and precision.

End-First Planning

Too often, projects grow larger, more complicated, and more stressful than necessary. A big part of the problem is that people focus on tasks before they focus on **outcomes**. Instead of asking, "What do I need to do today?", a more effective question is, *"What needs to be completed for this to be a success?"*

Event planner Rachel Carter, known for organizing large-scale corporate conferences, once found herself constantly overwhelmed by last-minute scrambling. No matter how much time she allocated, deadlines always seemed to sneak up. To regain control, she shifted her approach—starting with the finished event in mind and working backward to map out the necessary steps.

Instead of reacting to immediate demands, she worked toward fixed milestones, which eliminated the stress of last-minute rushes. Her new process forced her to prioritize the right steps, spot potential bottlenecks before they became emergencies, and set realistic deadlines based on how long things actually took—not on how quickly she wished they could be done.

One of the simplest ways to apply this strategy is the "Finish Cue"—before starting a project, take a moment to visualize the completed result. Then, work backward, identifying what needs to happen right before that point, and the step before that, all the way back to the present. Reverse planning forces clarity and turns time into an intentional sequence rather than a chaotic race.

The Buffer Wall: Building Time Safety Nets

Most people underestimate how long tasks will take. Deadlines are set based on best-case scenarios, assuming everything will go smoothly. But unexpected interruptions, delays, and complications are inevitable. Without extra space built into a schedule, even a small hiccup can cause everything to fall apart.

The solution is buffer time—intentionally adding extra time to every major task to absorb the unexpected. Studies on time perception show that people routinely underestimate task duration by 30-50%, meaning that without buffers, schedules collapse under the weight of reality.

One busy parent, juggling school drop-offs and early morning meetings, was constantly in a state of stress. Every morning was a race, with even minor delays—traffic, a forgotten lunchbox, a last-minute email—throwing the entire day off balance. To fix this, she started adding 20% extra time to every major part of her morning routine. Instead of aiming to leave home at 7:30 AM, she planned for 7:15. Instead of scheduling meetings immediately after school drop-offs, she left a 15-minute gap. The difference was immediate. With built-in flexibility, mornings became calmer, and she arrived at work feeling in control instead of frazzled.

This same approach works for any kind of work. By adding buffer time—whether for finishing reports, responding to emails, or preparing for meetings—stress decreases while productivity increases. A flexible schedule isn't inefficient; it's a strategic way to protect focus.

Another overlooked element of buffer time is the use of protected focus zones. These are designated blocks of time where no meetings, emails, or distractions are allowed. Just like a budget protects finances, a focus zone protects mental energy, ensuring that deep work happens without interruption.

By adding extra time cushions and protected focus periods, schedules become resilient instead of fragile, able to absorb delays without falling apart.

Purging False Urgency: Learning to Slow Down for Better Results

One of the biggest traps in time management is false urgency—the pressure to react immediately to every request, email, or notification.

Many tasks feel urgent when, in reality, they are simply loud distractions.

High performers learn to separate true urgency from unnecessary pressure. A simple but powerful tool for this is deliberate delay—intentionally pausing before reacting to anything that demands immediate attention.

A corporate finance manager, overwhelmed by constant emails and Slack messages, tested a simple experiment. Before responding to any request, he waited ten minutes. He quickly discovered that half of the "urgent" issues resolved themselves—either because someone else handled them or because they weren't important in the first place.

Over time, he began filtering tasks with three simple questions:

1. Is this truly urgent, or just demanding attention?
2. If I don't respond immediately, will there be catastrophic consequences?
3. Would delaying this task actually lead to a better decision?

This shift in approach freed up massive amounts of time. Instead of being stuck in reaction mode, he was able to focus on high-impact work without feeling like he was constantly racing.

Another strategy is prioritization by elimination. Instead of trying to do everything, focus on just the top three most important tasks each day. Everything beyond that can be scheduled for later, delegated, or ignored entirely. Cutting out unnecessary urgency leads to calmer, more intentional workdays, where focus remains sharp and progress stays steady.

Slowing down often produces better results. The constant push for speed leads to rushed decisions, half-baked ideas, and careless mistakes. When time pressure is artificially reduced, work becomes more thoughtful, creative, and effective.

Turning Time Into an Ally

Most people feel trapped by time, constantly racing against it. But by flipping the way time is approached—starting with the end goal, adding buffers, and eliminating fake urgency—it's possible to regain control.

Planning backward ensures that every step is intentional. Building buffer time creates flexibility that prevents stress. Eliminating false urgency stops the cycle of reacting to distractions instead of focusing on what matters.

Time isn't the enemy. When managed correctly, it becomes one of the greatest tools for focus and productivity.

Time Bend

Time doesn't move at the same speed for everyone. A single hour can feel like a fleeting moment or an endless stretch. The difference isn't in the number of minutes—it's in the way the brain processes those moments.

Athletes, artists, and high-performers have long understood this. They enter a state where time seems to slow, where their focus is absolute, and where every movement and decision feels natural and precise. This isn't luck. It's a skill. And anyone can learn it.

By understanding how the brain perceives time, it becomes possible to extend moments of deep focus, compress tedious tasks, and move through the day with a sense of effortless control. Work no longer feels like a race against the clock. Instead, it becomes an experience where time expands, allowing for clarity, creativity, and sustained attention.

Expanding Time Through Presence and Flow

Time stretches when the mind is fully engaged. When every detail is absorbed, and every action is intentional, the brain processes more information, making experiences feel longer and richer. This is why childhood summers seemed endless—every experience was new, and every moment was filled with curiosity. As routines become more predictable, the brain fast-tracks information, making time feel like it's slipping away.

The secret to slowing time isn't to do less. It's to engage more.

One of the most effective ways to achieve this is through deep work—uninterrupted periods of high-focus activity. Research by psychologist Mihaly Csikszentmihalyi on the state of "flow" found that when people are fully immersed in a challenging task, their perception of time shifts dramatically. They experience fewer distractions, work more efficiently, and often come out of a session feeling energized rather than drained.

A novelist struggling with creative blocks decided to test this principle. Instead of setting a strict writing schedule, he removed all clocks from his workspace and committed to writing until he naturally lost momentum. Without the distraction of time, he found himself entering deep work more quickly and staying in it longer. The hours melted away, and his productivity soared.

Flow is a trainable state. The more the mind is conditioned to enter it, the easier it becomes to sustain focus for extended periods. Now, this level of deep immersion isn't paradoxical to ultradian rhythms. The important thing to note is that these are all tools for you to explore. For me, deep immersion works better early in the day and then setting 90 minute work blocks is best for me post-lunch. Find your own style and remember that these are all just tools, not static musts.

. . .

Using Sound and Rhythm to Shape Time Perception

Sound is one of the most powerful yet overlooked tools for controlling time perception. The brain naturally syncs with external rhythms, meaning the right auditory environment can either extend focus or disrupt it entirely.

Music at around 60 beats per minute—roughly the rhythm of a calm heartbeat—has been shown to increase concentration and relaxation. This is why many deep-focus playlists feature ambient, classical, or instrumental music. Slower rhythms create a sense of spaciousness, while faster tempos can enhance bursts of short-term energy.

However, not all sounds are beneficial. The brain is wired to respond to unpredictable noises—notifications, background conversations, and sudden interruptions all fragment attention. By carefully curating an auditory environment, it's possible to guide focus rather than fight against distractions.

A professional dancer unknowingly applied this principle in her training. She discovered that certain types of music helped her memorize choreography faster, while others made her more prone to mistakes. When she extended this concept beyond dance—using specific music for writing, workouts, and even unwinding before bed—she gained a new level of control over her focus and energy levels throughout the day.

Rhythm is more than just sound. It's a tool for structuring time and making work feel fluid instead of forced.

Reframing Time to Reduce Stress and Increase Control

Time pressure can be one of the biggest barriers to focus. The constant feeling of racing against the clock creates anxiety, making it harder to enter deep work. The key to reversing this is reframing time —not as an enemy, but as an ally.

One approach is to use time constraints strategically. Instead of seeing deadlines as stress points, they can be transformed into motivators. A filmmaker working on a tight post-production schedule experimented with this by setting micro-deadlines—allocating fixed time slots to specific tasks rather than working against a looming, undefined deadline. By treating time as structured intervals rather than a vanishing resource, he felt more in control and completed his project ahead of schedule.

Another technique is to practice time dilation—mentally expanding moments by fully engaging with them. A painter struggling to complete a large-scale commission started approaching each brushstroke as a meditation. Instead of rushing, he slowed down, focusing entirely on the movement of his hand and the texture of the paint. As a result, his sense of time stretched, and what once felt overwhelming became an experience of total immersion.

The way time is perceived influences the way work is done. By shifting from a mindset of scarcity ("I don't have enough time") to one of abundance ("I control how I experience time"), it becomes easier to focus deeply and work with greater ease.

Mastering Time Perception for Lasting Focus

The most productive people don't have more time. They experience time differently. By engaging fully in the present moment, using sound to shape focus, and reframing time to reduce pressure, it's possible to unlock a level of concentration that makes every hour count.

Time isn't something to fight against—it's something to flow with. The more control there is over time perception, the easier it becomes to sustain focus, work more effectively, and feel energized rather than drained at the end of the day.

Your Review Can Change Someone's Life

"You can't do big things if you're constantly distracted by small ones."
– Anonymous

People who give without expecting anything in return live more fulfilled lives. Let's make a difference together.

Would you help someone just like you—someone determined to reclaim their focus but unsure where to start?

My mission is simple: to help people cut through the noise, master deep work, and unlock their full potential. But to reach more people, I need your help.

Most readers choose books based on reviews. Your review—just a few words—could be the reason someone takes the leap to break free from distraction.

It costs nothing and takes less than a minute, but it could change someone's journey. Your review could help…

- … one more writer finally finish their book.
- … one more student study without getting sidetracked.
- … one more entrepreneur build a thriving business.
- … one more professional reclaim their time and energy.
- … one more person break free from the cycle of distractions.

To make a difference, simply go to whichever platform that you purchased this book from and leave a review now.

If you love helping others, you're my kind of person. Thank you for being part of this movement toward better focus, deeper work, and a life well-lived.

Jordan Cross

Chapter 6

The Deep Work Dive

Deep work is the state where focus is at its peak, creativity flourishes, and real progress happens. It's the opposite of surface-level productivity, where tasks are constantly interrupted, and attention is scattered.

This chapter isn't about working longer—it's about working deeper. When you master deep work, an hour of focused effort can accomplish more than an entire day of multitasking. The challenge isn't just about finding time; it's about creating an environment and mindset that makes deep work the default instead of the exception.

By setting up structured time for undisturbed focus, using physical and mental signals to reinforce commitment, and eliminating digital temptations, deep work becomes second nature. And when practiced consistently, it rewires the brain for sustained attention, unlocking a level of clarity and efficiency that most people never experience.

Dive Prep

Deep work doesn't happen by chance—it requires structure. Without preparation, distractions creep in, pulling attention away before real focus can take hold.

Think of it like swimming in a cluttered pool. If you don't clear the surface first, every stroke is interrupted. The same applies to focus—without dedicated time, clear signals, and a distraction-free space, deep work remains out of reach.

Structuring Time for Deep Work

The first step to mastering deep work is protecting time for it. Without dedicated focus blocks, attention will always be at the mercy of interruptions, notifications, and the constant pull of shallow tasks.

One of the most effective strategies is establishing **sacred hours**—non-negotiable time slots dedicated solely to deep work. These sessions should be scheduled when the brain is naturally primed for focus. For many, this is early in the morning before distractions pile up. For others, it might be late at night when the world quiets down. The key is consistency. When deep work is treated as sacred, it stops feeling like an optional luxury and becomes a daily habit.

A well-known author who struggled with procrastination put this principle into practice. He committed to writing for two hours every morning—no emails, no phone, no distractions. Within 90 days, he completed a manuscript that had been stalled for years. The difference wasn't that he worked harder; it was that he worked deeper, giving his mind the uninterrupted space to generate ideas and refine them.

Deep work flourishes in well-defined time blocks. The challenge is not just setting them up, but defending them against the forces of distraction.

Using Signals to Lock Into Focus

Creating a distraction-free environment isn't just about external control—it's also about training the mind to recognize when it's time to enter a deep work state. This is where **signal switches** become powerful. These are small, deliberate cues that tell the brain, "It's time to focus."

One of the simplest and most effective signal switches is closing the door. It's a physical barrier that tells both the outside world and the subconscious mind that focus is now the priority. Another is putting on noise-canceling headphones—even if no music is playing. It signals to the brain that external stimuli are being blocked out.

A corporate manager struggling to carve out time for high-level strategic work started using this method. Every afternoon at 2 p.m., he put on his headphones, turned his chair away from his desk, and placed a "Do Not Disturb" sign on his monitor. His team quickly learned not to interrupt him during these sessions, and over time, the simple act of putting on his headphones became an automatic trigger for his mind to shift into deep work mode.

Signal switches act as environmental triggers that eliminate the need for willpower. When repeated consistently, they create a conditioned response that makes transitioning into focus effortless.

Eliminating Digital Distractions for Deep Work

One of the greatest threats to deep work is digital noise. The very devices designed to enhance productivity often sabotage it by flooding attention with notifications, messages, and infinite streams of content. The solution isn't just about self-control—it's about creating a system where focus is the default.

One of the most effective methods is tech isolation—physically and digitally separating deep work from distraction sources. Putting a phone in another room, using app blockers, or switching to airplane mode creates a boundary that prevents temptation. Another strategy is analog flipping—switching to paper notebooks, whiteboards, or physical books to break free from the digital vortex.

In 2012, Cal Newport, was researching the impact of deep work on productivity. He found himself constantly interrupted by emails, meetings, and notifications, making it difficult to focus on complex coding and academic writing. Determined to reclaim his concentration, he implemented a strict "deep work" schedule, during which he turned off his Wi-Fi, put his phone in another room, and worked in uninterrupted blocks of time. The results were transformative. Not only did his efficiency double, but he was able to produce high-quality research at an accelerated pace, while also reducing stress caused by constant digital interruptions. His experience led to the development of the "Deep Work" philosophy, which has since helped thousands of professionals escape the trap of distraction and achieve peak focus.

The modern world is designed to fracture attention. By proactively creating barriers between deep work and digital interruptions, it's possible to reclaim focus and produce work of far greater depth and quality.

Unlocking the Power of Deep Work

The ability to work deeply isn't a talent—it's a skill. Like any skill, it strengthens with practice. The more time spent in deep work, the easier it becomes to enter and sustain it.

By structuring sacred hours, using signal switches to transition into focus, and eliminating digital distractions, deep work stops feeling like an occasional burst of productivity and starts becoming a natural state of high performance.

Most people never experience the true power of deep work. But for those who do, it changes everything—from the quality of their output to the clarity of their thinking. The challenge is simple: Are you willing to go deep?

Immersion Keys

Starting deep work is one thing—staying in it is another. Even in an ideal environment, where distractions are minimized and time is protected, the mind will still resist focus. Boredom creeps in, motivation dips, and suddenly, that intense state of flow feels out of reach. The key to sustained deep work isn't just removing interruptions—it's making the work itself deeply engaging.

To keep focus locked in, three things matter most: challenge, feedback, and stakes. The mind thrives when tasks are difficult but achievable, when progress is measurable, and when there's something on the line. When these three elements are in place, focus stops feeling like a struggle and starts feeling automatic.

The Power of Challenge

Have you ever noticed how time flies when you're doing something difficult yet exciting? Whether it's an intense workout, a puzzle that's just within reach of being solved, or a competitive game, challenge sharpens attention. Deep work thrives on difficulty. When something is too easy, the brain disengages. When something is too hard, it triggers frustration. But when a task is at the right level of difficulty—just beyond your current ability but within reach with effort—it creates what researchers call the *flow state*.

This sweet spot, known as the *stretch zone*, is where deep work becomes effortless. The mind is fully engaged because the task demands it. This is why world-class athletes, musicians, and artists constantly push their limits. They don't just repeat what they already know—they take on challenges that force them to grow.

To maintain immersion in deep work, choose tasks that are slightly beyond your current abilities. If a task feels tedious, increase its difficulty. If it feels overwhelming, break it down into manageable steps. The key is to balance challenge with competence—enough pressure to demand full concentration, but not so much that it triggers frustration.

When a task is too easy, focus slips. This is why repetitive admin work, dull meetings, and mindless busywork feel draining—they don't require deep thinking. The brain disengages, and distractions become more tempting. In contrast, challenging work pulls attention in naturally.

Failure is also a key part of the process. In high-performance fields, failure isn't seen as a setback—it's a sign of pushing limits. Olympic athletes, elite chess players, and top engineers don't avoid failure; they use it to measure progress. If you're never failing, you're not pushing hard enough.

When professional climber Alex Honnold was training for his historic free solo climb of El Capitan, he didn't just practice the same routes over and over. He deliberately tackled harder and harder sections, increasing the difficulty until it forced total focus. He made deep work inevitable by ensuring the challenge was always just beyond his current ability.

For deep work to feel immersive, find your version of Honnold's approach. Whether you're writing, coding, designing, or solving problems, constantly raise the bar just enough to keep the mind fully engaged.

The Feedback Loop

Progress fuels deep work. One reason focus fades is that progress is invisible. When you're doing deep work, the results often take time to show. This can make it hard to stay motivated—especially in long-term projects. The solution is immediate feedback.

The human brain craves progress. This is why video games are so addictive—they provide constant feedback through scores, levels, and rewards. But deep work, if left unstructured, often lacks this immediate reinforcement. To stay immersed, you need a way to measure progress in real time.

Creating small, visible wins throughout a work session keeps focus locked in. If you're writing, track word count. If you're coding, log completed sections. If you're designing, take snapshots of your progress. Seeing progress fuels motivation, making it easier to stay in deep work mode.

Setting small, meaningful checkpoints makes long projects feel manageable. Instead of working on a vague goal like "write a book," break it into micro-milestones: write 500 words, complete one chapter, revise three paragraphs. Each milestone creates a sense of completion, which fuels continued focus.

Many high-performers use progress tracking systems to stay engaged. Writers track word count or pages completed. Athletes log workouts and performance metrics. Software engineers track completed features. By making progress visible, deep work becomes self-reinforcing.

A professional illustrator struggling with motivation started using a sketch-by-sketch system. Instead of forcing himself to complete full pieces, he focused on drawing one key element at a time—a single hand, a facial expression, a texture. Each micro-win built momentum, keeping him immersed for hours at a time.

Risk & Stakes: Why Deadlines and Pressure Sharpen Focus

Most people think distractions are the biggest threat to deep work. But often, the real problem is a lack of urgency. When there's no reason to focus now, the brain drifts. This is why deadlines, social accountability, and meaningful stakes create instant immersion.

A study on procrastination found that people who set clear deadlines with consequences were far more likely to complete their work on time. Deadlines force commitment, creating a natural sense of urgency.

One of the fastest ways to create stakes is to tell someone your goal. Social pressure activates accountability, making it harder to procrastinate. This is why many top performers announce projects publicly before they're finished—once people are watching, there's no turning back.

Research shows that humans are wired to avoid loss more than they seek gains. This is why attaching a real consequence to failure can boost focus. Some ways to do this include:

- Betting money on your deadline—if you miss it, donate the amount.
- Setting a public commitment—if you fail, admit it online.
- Creating a rule: No social media or entertainment until the task is done.

When there's something at stake, deep work becomes easier.

When a small startup faced an impossible deadline for a product launch, they made one strategic move—they publicly committed to a release date in a major tech publication. The moment the announcement was live, their focus skyrocketed. With the pressure on, deep work became the only option. They met the deadline, and the launch was a success.

Making Deep Work Effortless

The hack to prolonged deep work is by designing an environment where focus becomes inevitable. By setting the right level of challenge, creating instant feedback loops, and raising the stakes, you make it easier to stay immersed than to drift into distraction.

Output Burst

Deep work isn't just about spending long hours in concentration—it's about making those hours count. The difference between spinning your wheels and making real progress comes down to how efficiently you structure your work sessions.

Highly productive individuals follow three core principles: grouping similar tasks to avoid attention residue, drafting quickly without overanalyzing, and tracking progress in a way that fuels motivation. By mastering these techniques, you can turn every deep work session into a powerhouse of productivity.

Batching for Maximum Efficiency

Task-switching is one of the biggest focus killers. Every time you move from one type of task to another—say, writing an email, then answering a phone call, then returning to deep work—your brain has to recalibrate. This cognitive lag is called *attention residue*, and it can drastically reduce your productivity.

Batching similar tasks together eliminates this inefficiency. Instead of responding to emails throughout the day, set aside a specific time to go through all of them at once. Instead of jumping between writing and research, separate those activities into different sessions. The less often your brain has to reset, the more energy you have for meaningful work.

Ray Edwards' Content Creation Approach

Ray Edwards, a renowned copywriter and author, has long preached the benefits of batching. He developed a system to write an entire week's worth of blog posts in just one hour. How? He dedicates a single, distraction-free session to writing—no emails, no notifications, just deep focus. By eliminating interruptions and riding the momentum of a singular task, he maximizes efficiency without sacrificing quality.

His method proves a simple truth: when you batch your tasks, you work smarter—not harder.

Drafting Without Hesitation

One of the biggest mistakes people make during deep work is trying to perfect their output as they go. They second-guess every sentence, refine every paragraph, and agonize over tiny details. But the most productive people in any creative field know that the first draft is never the final product.

The key is to separate *creation* from *editing*. The goal of the first draft isn't to be flawless—it's to get ideas onto the page. Once the foundation is there, refining becomes much easier. Writers, designers, and even entrepreneurs benefit from embracing an imperfect but fast-first-pass approach.

Ihara Saikaku's Prolific Writing Feat

In 1684, Japanese poet Ihara Saikaku set out to push his creative limits. Over the course of a single day and night, he composed a staggering 23,500 haikai verses. While this was an extreme example of rapid drafting, it demonstrated the power of removing hesitation. Instead of overthinking, he let creativity flow freely, refining his work afterward.

The lesson? When you prioritize speed in early drafts, you tap into deeper creative reserves and overcome the perfectionist trap.

Tracking Progress to Sustain Momentum

Have you ever worked for hours on something but felt like you had nothing to show for it? That feeling kills motivation. The human brain craves visible progress—whether it's crossing an item off a to-do list or watching a progress bar fill up.

Tracking progress in tangible ways reinforces the habit of deep work. It transforms an abstract process into something measurable, making it easier to stay engaged and push forward. Drawing boxes on a physical A4 or A3 paper with each box signifying 1 day works wonders. This was the tool I used to quit pornography and a lot of unhealthy habits when I was crawling out of my depressive period.

If you're someone who loves tech tools, there are many apps available today to help you track your progress. There's apps to quit smoking, quit alcohol, quit pornography. Find the method that works for you. The physical sensation of ticking off a box on the paper felt incredible for me, as silly as it sounds.

Neil Pasricha's "1000 Awesome Things" Project

Neil Pasricha, author and blogger, set out to write about *1000 Awesome Things*—one every weekday for 1000 days. By breaking his massive goal into small, achievable steps, he kept himself motivated. Each completed post wasn't just another item checked off a list—it was a visible sign of progress. This tracking system kept him accountable, ultimately leading to a bestselling book.

His success highlights an important takeaway: small, trackable milestones fuel long-term discipline.

How to Implement These Strategies in Your Work

To make your deep work sessions more productive, integrate these three principles into your routine:

1. **Batch similar tasks** to minimize the cognitive drain of frequent task-switching.
2. **Draft quickly without self-editing** to build momentum and avoid overthinking.
3. **Track visible progress** to maintain motivation and reinforce effort.

When combined, these strategies transform deep work from an exhausting endeavor into a streamlined, rewarding process. With practice, you'll find yourself completing high-impact work in less time, unlocking new levels of focus and efficiency.

Chapter 7

The Distraction Shield

The modern world is designed to steal your focus. Your phone lights up with notifications, your inbox overflows with unread emails, and the pull of endless scrolling keeps your brain in a constant state of stimulation. The result? Your attention is scattered, your productivity suffers, and deep work becomes nearly impossible.

The solution isn't to rely on willpower. It's to build a **distraction shield**—a system that minimizes digital intrusions, neutralizes unnecessary pings, and allows you to work with clarity. This chapter explores how to fortify your focus by taming your apps, reducing screen interference, and restructuring how you handle email.

Tech Armor

Your phone isn't just a communication tool—it's a finely tuned distraction machine. Every app, notification, and algorithm is designed to pull you in, fragmenting your attention and making deep work feel impossible. Without realizing it, you may be caught in a cycle where your phone dictates your focus instead of the other way around.

The key isn't to throw away your phone—it's to strip away its power over your attention. Small but deliberate changes, like turning your screen to grayscale, limiting notifications, or deleting the most distracting apps, can dramatically reduce mindless engagement. Instead of fighting temptation every time you pick up your phone, you remove the temptation entirely.

Many high performers—including CEOs, authors, and creatives—take this even further. They design tech-free zones, use distraction blockers, and schedule strict "no-phone" hours to create an environment where deep work can thrive. The less power your devices have over you, the more control you regain over your time, focus, and productivity.

Taming the App Overload

Smartphones are engineered for addiction. Every feature—colorful icons, endless scroll feeds, red notification badges—triggers dopamine, keeping you hooked. The average person picks up their phone **344 times per day**, often without realizing it. To break free, you need to make apps work for you, not against you.

One of the simplest but most effective tricks is **grayscale mode**—turning your phone's display to black and white. Color is a powerful attention magnet; dulling it reduces the urge to check notifications mindlessly. A study by NYU researchers found that users spent significantly less time on social media when their screens were in grayscale.

Another approach is the **five-app purge** rule. Identify the five most distracting apps on your phone and delete them. If that feels too extreme, remove them from your home screen so they aren't the first thing you see when you unlock your device.

Dimming the Digital Glow

Screens aren't just distracting—they disrupt sleep, overstimulate the brain, and fragment attention. One of the biggest culprits is **blue light**, which suppresses melatonin and keeps the brain in a heightened state of alertness.

Switching your device to **night mode** reduces this effect. Most phones, tablets, and laptops have built-in features that shift screens to warmer tones in the evening. But for true focus protection, it's not just about color—it's about reducing overall screen exposure.

In 2018, Tristan Harris, a former Google design ethicist and founder of the Center for Humane Technology, spoke about how tech companies deliberately engineer distractions. Harris himself struggled with overuse and tested various strategies to regain focus. One of the most effective? Turning off all notifications and implementing a strict "no-screen" hour before bed. This simple habit improved his sleep, boosted his cognitive function, and allowed for uninterrupted deep work the next morning.

Another common focus killer? **Mindless scrolling**. Platforms like Instagram, TikTok, and YouTube are designed to be endless—there's no natural stopping point. To combat this, try **scroll blocking**—set a rule that you'll only check social media on a computer, never on your phone. This creates intentional friction, making it easier to avoid rabbit holes. There are also a lot of app extensions that allow you to install and remove your home page completely when you enter the website.

Do whatever it takes. Try it! It is amazing how much more focused we become when our brain no longer seeks rewards from meaningless scrolling and tapping.

Mastering Email for Deep Work

Replying to emails is often treated as an urgent task, but in reality, most messages don't require immediate attention. The constant checking and responding create a cycle of reactive work, where you spend more time managing emails than doing meaningful tasks.

One of the simplest solutions is email batching—checking your inbox at set times instead of letting it interrupt you throughout the day. Many high-performing professionals use the twice-daily rule, where they check and respond to emails only at 10 AM and 4 PM. This prevents email from hijacking the most productive hours of the day.

To streamline the process further:

- **Use filters** to automatically sort non-urgent emails.
- **Unsubscribe** from newsletters and promotions that clutter your inbox.
- **Reply concisely**—aim for three sentences or less.

Tim Ferriss, entrepreneur and author of *The 4-Hour Workweek*, took this strategy even further. He made a radical shift—checking email only once per week. His rule? "If it's truly urgent, people will find another way to reach me." While this extreme approach may not be feasible for everyone, it underscores an important lesson: email should serve your work, not the other way around.

Another example is Sheryl Sandberg, former COO of Meta, who implemented a strict policy: she never checked email first thing in the morning. Instead, she used the early hours for focused work, knowing that once she opened her inbox, she'd be pulled into a reactive mindset. This small habit helped her maintain control over her schedule, ensuring that deep work came first.

Email should be a tool, not a trap. By controlling when and how you engage with it, you prevent it from dictating your attention.

Building a Lasting Distraction Shield

Distraction-proofing your work isn't about discipline—it's about designing an environment that makes focus easy. By reducing digital noise, minimizing unnecessary alerts, and restructuring how you interact with screens and email, you build a defense system that protects your attention.

Once you've tamed digital distractions, the next challenge is creating a "people guard". It is time to learn how to say "NO" to others without guilt.

People Guard

Conversations, requests, and meetings can quietly consume hours of your time, leaving little room for meaningful work. A simple question from a colleague, a family member seeking attention, or a last-minute meeting invite can pull you away from what truly matters.

Interruptions don't just steal minutes; they break flow—the mental state where your best work happens. Earlier in this book, we explored how even brief distractions force your brain to reset, reducing efficiency by up to 40%, as found in a 2021 study from the University of California. How do you guard your time when other people are the distraction?

The solution isn't to shut the world out entirely—it's about training others to respect your focus. This chapter explores three essential strategies: using verbal scripts to handle interruptions, leveraging physical cues to signal when you're unavailable, and slashing unnecessary meetings that drain productivity.

No Scripts: Saying No Without Guilt

Many people struggle to say no, even when they know an interruption will derail their work. There's a natural tendency to be polite, to avoid seeming dismissive, or to fear missing out. But if you don't set boundaries, interruptions will keep happening.

Instead of an abrupt "I'm busy," a well-crafted response can decline interruptions without damaging relationships:

- **The Polite Dodge:** "I'd love to chat, but now isn't a great time. Let's catch up later."
- **The Time Claim:** "I'm deep in something right now, but I'll check in when I'm free."
- **The Yes Delay:** "Let me finish this first, then I'll get back to you."
- **The Firm Line:** "I can't step away right now. Let's touch base later."

When delivered with confidence, these responses help train colleagues, family members, or friends to respect your focus without shutting them out entirely.

How a Teacher Took Control

Lisa Caldwell, a high school teacher, used to be overwhelmed by constant interruptions from both students and colleagues. Staff would drop by her classroom for casual chats, and students frequently interrupted her planning time with questions that could wait. She realized that if she didn't take control, she would never reclaim her focus.

Her solution? She implemented a simple system. During planning periods, she placed a small sign on her desk that read "Lesson Planning in Progress." When approached, she politely but firmly said, "I'll be free after class—we can talk then."

Within weeks, interruptions dropped dramatically. Her students learned to write their questions down instead of asking immediately, and colleagues began respecting her focused work time. By setting clear verbal and visual boundaries, she reclaimed hours of deep work every week.

Signal Props: Using Physical Cues to Block Interruptions

Sometimes, words aren't enough. If people see that you're at your desk or in the room, they assume you're available. That's why physical signals can be even more effective than verbal ones.

Think of it like a traffic light: Green means go, yellow means wait, and red means stop. You can create a similar system in your workspace using subtle, non-verbal cues that make it clear when you're not to be disturbed.

- **Headphones as a Barrier** – Wearing large headphones (even without music) is a universal "do not disturb" signal.
- **A Visible Focus Zone** – A simple "Deep Work in Progress" sign on your desk can make a difference.
- **Desk Positioning** – Facing away from common traffic areas reduces interruptions.
- **Body Language** – Avoiding eye contact when working makes people less likely to engage.

Using Headphones to Guard His Time

Bestselling author Mark Dawson struggled to focus while writing in public spaces. Friends and acquaintances often interrupted him for casual chats, pulling him out of his creative flow.

His solution was simple but effective: he started wearing large, noise-canceling headphones—even when he wasn't listening to music. The moment he put them on, people assumed he was deep in work and stopped trying to start conversations.

The result? He finished his book ahead of schedule. This small, non-verbal signal became his secret weapon against distractions.

Eliminating Time-Wasting Meetings

Meetings are often the greatest productivity drain in the workplace. They're scheduled automatically, drag on too long, and frequently include people who don't need to be there. Most professionals spend 15+ hours per week in meetings, yet studies show that nearly half of that time is wasted.

To reclaim your time, take control of meetings rather than letting them control you:

- **15-Minute Max** – If a meeting lasts longer than 15 minutes, it's often poorly structured.
- **Agenda Lock** – No agenda? No meeting. Every meeting should have a purpose.
- **The Stand Rule** – Standing meetings keep people focused and efficient.
- **No Invite, No Show** – If you're unsure why you were invited, ask before attending—or skip it entirely.

· · ·

The Team That Slashed Meetings and Got More Done

At Airbnb, CEO Brian Chesky noticed that meetings were eating into deep work time. Employees were constantly pulled into discussions, leaving little room for actual execution. To address this, the company cut all default meetings over 30 minutes and replaced long status updates with brief, daily stand-up huddles.

The change was immediate: teams had more focused work hours, decisions were made faster, and productivity skyrocketed. By simply reducing unnecessary meetings, Airbnb freed up hundreds of hours per month across the company.

Mastering the Art of People Guarding

While collaboration and communication are valuable, unnecessary interruptions can erode deep work time. The good news? You have control.

- **Use verbal scripts** to politely decline interruptions.
- **Leverage physical signals** like headphones or desk signs to create a non-verbal boundary.
- **Take control of meetings** by setting strict limits, ensuring clear agendas, and declining unnecessary invites.

Train the people around you to respect your time. By implementing these small but powerful changes, you reclaim control over your attention, paving the way for sharper concentration, higher-quality work, and a life where deep work is the default.

Mind Wall

Some of the most powerful distractions aren't external. They come from within—fleeting thoughts, worries, and mental detours that quietly pull attention away from what matters. Unlike notifications or noisy environments, internal distractions don't announce themselves. They creep in unnoticed, hijacking focus before we even realize we've been pulled off track.

You sit down to work, but a random thought pops up about an unfinished task. A worry about tomorrow's deadline nudges its way into your head. Before you know it, you're deep in an unrelated train of thought, far from the work you intended to do. This happens to everyone, but the difference between those who stay focused and those who struggle isn't whether their minds wander—it's how quickly they recognize and redirect their attention.

Internal distractions can't be eliminated completely, but they can be controlled. The key is developing the ability to catch mental drift early, reset focus when it slips, and contain nagging worries so they don't take over. These three strategies—thought catching, quick resets, and worry management—create a mental firewall that keeps distractions from running the show.

Catching the Drift Before It Becomes a Spiral

Distractions often follow a pattern. Some people lose focus when a task feels overwhelming. Others get derailed by boredom or restlessness. Understanding what triggers mental drift makes it easier to stop.

Noticing distraction early is crucial. The longer the mind wanders, the harder it is to return. One effective method is to pause and observe thoughts throughout the day. Each time attention drifts, take note of what caused it. Was it an unfinished responsibility? A random idea? The urge to check your phone? Recognizing these moments strengthens awareness and improves the ability to stay on track.

For immediate redirection, a physical action can serve as a reset. Something as simple as tapping a desk, rubbing hands together, or shifting posture can break the cycle of distraction and pull attention back. Another approach is writing down intrusive thoughts. Keeping a small notebook nearby allows distractions to be acknowledged without engaging with them. This prevents the mental loops that often lead to prolonged focus breaks.

How a Designer Reclaimed His Attention

Graphic designer Daniel Burka struggled with staying focused on complex projects. His mind would frequently jump to unanswered emails, upcoming deadlines, or half-finished ideas, making deep work nearly impossible.

To combat this, he started keeping a small journal next to his desk. Each time a distracting thought popped up, instead of acting on it, he wrote it down and continued working. If the thought was important, he could address it later; if it wasn't, it lost its power the moment it was recorded.

Within weeks, he noticed a difference. His focus became sharper, and he was able to sustain deep work sessions without constantly feeling pulled in different directions. The simple act of acknowledging distractions without indulging them gave him control over his attention.

The Fastest Way to Reset a Wandering Mind

Even with strong awareness, focus still slips. The key is how quickly it recovers. The longer mental drift lasts, the harder it is to regain momentum. That's why having a fast reset strategy is crucial.

One of the simplest and most effective resets is **movement**. Standing up and stretching for just 30 seconds disrupts mental inertia, improves circulation, and refreshes cognitive function. A structured approach like the **20-20-20 rule** can also help: every 20 minutes, look at something 20 feet away for 20 seconds. This not only relieves eye strain but also prevents mental fatigue from prolonged concentration.

Hydration plays an important role in focus too. Mild dehydration has been shown to impair cognitive function, slow reaction time, and increase fatigue. Drinking a glass of water can provide an instant mental boost.

For immediate clarity, a single deep breath works wonders. Inhaling slowly, holding for a moment, and then exhaling fully helps reset stress levels and re-engage focus.

A Nurse's Mid-Shift Reboot

Carla Hall, a critical care nurse, faced constant high-pressure situations. By midday, her mental clarity would start to fade. The weight of decision-making, rapid problem-solving, and patient care demands took a toll.

Determined to stay sharp throughout her shifts, she created a simple **reset ritual**. Every time she washed her hands, she took one deep breath and rolled her shoulders back, using that moment as a mental refresh.

This small habit made a significant impact. She felt more present with her patients, experienced fewer lapses in concentration, and noticed a drop in end-of-shift exhaustion. What started as a simple breath practice became a built-in focus reset that kept her engaged even in the most chaotic environments.

Containing Worries So They Don't Steal Mental Bandwidth

Not all distractions are momentary. Some linger—unfinished tasks, upcoming deadlines, unresolved anxieties. These background concerns can pull focus away, even when there's no immediate action to take.

The brain constantly seeks closure. If something feels unresolved, it will keep surfacing, demanding attention. Ignoring it doesn't help. The more you try to push a worry aside, the stronger it becomes. The solution is to give it a place to go.

One of the simplest ways to do this is through a **worry dump**—writing down every lingering thought, unanswered question, or undone task. This isn't a to-do list; it's a mental unloading. The goal isn't to solve anything in the moment but to offload it so the mind can let go.

Another approach is **time-boxing worry**. Instead of allowing nagging thoughts to pop up throughout the day, set a five-minute window later to revisit them. This reassures the brain that concerns won't be ignored, reducing their urgency in the moment. Some people find it helpful to physically remove written worries—ripping up the page, tossing it away, or burning it as a symbolic act of closure.

A Parent's Panic Purge

Sarah Evans, a working mother, constantly struggled with mental clutter. Her attention was split between work responsibilities, household tasks, and parenting concerns. Even when she tried to focus, her mind would race through an endless stream of unfinished to-dos.

Desperate for a solution, she started a **morning worry dump**. Before beginning her workday, she spent five minutes writing down every stressor, incomplete task, and lingering thought. Once it was on paper, she closed the notebook and moved on.

Her mind felt clearer, and she was able to focus on work without the constant pull of unrelated thoughts. Over time, this small habit transformed her productivity.

Training the Mind to Stay on Track

Focus isn't just about avoiding external distractions. It's about building an internal system that keeps attention locked in, even when the mind wants to wander.

By noticing mental drift early, resetting focus quickly, and offloading nagging concerns, it's possible to create an unshakable focus system.

When the mind is no longer a battlefield of competing thoughts, focus shifts from being a constant struggle to a sustainable strength—one that powers better work, deeper creativity, and greater mental clarity.

Chapter 8

The Focus Fuel Mix

What you eat and drink directly impacts your ability to focus, sustain deep work, and think clearly. The brain is a high-energy organ, consuming nearly 20% of the body's total energy despite making up only a small fraction of body weight. This means that what you fuel it with can either enhance or undermine cognitive performance.

The right nutrition sharpens attention, stabilizes mood, and prevents mental fatigue. On the other hand, poor dietary choices—such as sugar spikes, dehydration, and caffeine misuse—can lead to brain fog, sluggishness, and focus crashes.

Understanding how to optimize food, hydration, and stimulants like caffeine is essential for maintaining peak concentration throughout the day. This section explores practical, science-backed nutrition strategies to keep the mind sharp and fully engaged.

Food Edge

The brain runs primarily on glucose, but not all sources of glucose are equal. A steady, slow-releasing fuel source keeps attention stable, while rapid spikes lead to focus crashes. The key is choosing foods that sustain energy without creating rollercoaster effects.

Sugary snacks and refined carbs—such as white bread, candy, and pastries—provide quick but fleeting bursts of energy. The initial high is followed by a sharp drop, leaving the mind foggy and sluggish. In contrast, foods rich in protein, fiber, and healthy fats provide a slow, sustained release of glucose, keeping the brain fueled without sudden crashes.

For example, research has shown that nuts, eggs, and whole grains promote steady cognitive performance. Almonds, walnuts, and cashews contain healthy fats and protein that help sustain energy for hours. Eggs are rich in choline, a key nutrient for brain function and memory retention.

Elon Musk, known for his grueling work schedule, once relied on candy bars and Diet Coke to power through long hours. But after experiencing energy crashes and struggling with sustained focus, he switched to a diet that prioritized protein and healthy fats. Within weeks, he reported better mental clarity and improved sustained focus throughout the day. His experience reflects what nutritional science has confirmed—what you eat has a direct impact on how long and how well you can concentrate.

Hydration

Even mild dehydration—just a 2% drop in body water levels—can cause mental fatigue, sluggish thinking, and impaired concentration. The brain relies on adequate hydration to deliver nutrients, regulate temperature, and maintain cognitive function.

Despite its importance, many people go hours without drinking enough water, relying on coffee or energy drinks instead. Caffeine doesn't replace water—in fact, it can lead to dehydration if consumed in excess.

The solution is consistent, strategic hydration. Experts recommend drinking small amounts of water frequently rather than chugging large amounts all at once. A good rule of thumb is 8 ounces per hour during the workday.

Adding electrolytes such as sodium and potassium can further enhance focus and prevent dehydration-related fatigue. Coconut water, electrolyte tablets, or a pinch of sea salt in water can be helpful for those who sweat frequently or drink excessive amounts of caffeine.

LeBron James, one of the greatest basketball players of all time, understands the importance of hydration. He reportedly drinks a gallon of water per day to maintain peak physical and mental performance. During a 2014 NBA Finals game, James suffered severe cramping due to dehydration, forcing him to leave the court. After that experience, he revamped his hydration strategy, ensuring he consumed steady amounts of water throughout the day rather than waiting until he felt thirsty.

While most people aren't performing under stadium lights, the principle applies to everyone—waiting until you feel thirsty means you're already dehydrated, and your focus is likely suffering.

Caffeine

Caffeine is one of the most widely used cognitive enhancers in the world. When used correctly, it boosts alertness, enhances concentration, and improves mood. But when misused, it can lead to energy crashes, jitteriness, and disrupted sleep—all of which harm focus in the long run.

The key to maximizing caffeine's benefits while avoiding its downsides is timing and moderation. Studies show that delaying the first dose of caffeine by 90 minutes after waking up prevents the typical mid-morning energy crash.

Additionally, caffeine should be paired with food to avoid spiking cortisol and blood sugar levels. Drinking coffee on an empty stomach may lead to short-term alertness but long-term energy depletion.

For those prone to caffeine-related anxiety, switching to tea—which contains L-theanine, a natural compound that promotes calm focus—can provide a smoother, sustained energy boost without the jittery side effects.

James Hoffman, a world-renowned coffee expert and former World Barista Champion, once experimented with different caffeine dosages and consumption methods to optimize focus. He found that drinking smaller, more frequent doses of coffee throughout the day rather than one large morning cup led to smoother energy levels and better concentration. By understanding how caffeine affects the body, he adjusted his intake for consistent mental clarity rather than short bursts of stimulation followed by crashes. His takeaway? Caffeine should be a tool, not a crutch. Once again, what might work for you could be very different.

Optimizing Your Focus Fuel Strategy

The brain is an engine, and what you put into it determines how well it runs. Small changes in food, hydration, and caffeine intake can create significant improvements in concentration, energy levels, and mental endurance.

- Prioritize slow-releasing energy sources. Nuts, eggs, and whole grains keep the brain fueled without energy crashes.
- Drink consistently. Even mild dehydration impairs focus, so small, frequent sips of water make a difference.
- Use caffeine strategically. Delay the first cup, pair it with food, and consider switching to tea for a smoother effect.

With the right fuel, distractions fade, deep work becomes easier, and focus becomes effortless. What you consume today determines how well you'll think tomorrow—so choose wisely.

Move Spark

The body and mind are deeply connected. While most people think of focus as purely mental, physical movement plays a key role in sustaining deep concentration. Studies have shown that even brief movement can dramatically enhance cognitive performance by increasing blood flow, reducing mental fatigue, and improving mood.

When the body is stagnant for too long, circulation slows, oxygen supply to the brain decreases, and mental energy dips. This is why long periods of sitting can lead to sluggishness, brain fog, and reduced productivity. But the good news? Just a few minutes of movement can reset focus, improve mental clarity, and restore energy levels.

This section explores three simple but powerful ways to use movement as a focus enhancer—short bursts of intense activity, targeted stretching to relieve tension, and walking as a tool for creative thinking.

Energizing the Brain in Seconds

High-intensity movement—especially in short bursts—can jolt the brain into a state of heightened alertness. When you engage in quick, explosive movements like jumping jacks, stair sprints, or a 5-minute run, your heart rate increases, pumping more oxygen to the brain. This leads to a release of norepinephrine, a neurotransmitter associated with attention and mental sharpness.

The effects are almost immediate. Just 30 seconds of physical activity can clear mental fog and improve focus for the next hour. This is why many high-performers incorporate quick movement breaks into their workday to reset attention and sustain deep focus.

During the early 2000s, a customer service clerk at a New York-based insurance firm struggled with midday fatigue. Hours of desk work drained her energy, making it difficult to concentrate on calls and paperwork. On a whim, she began sprinting up a flight of office stairs every time she felt herself zoning out. Within days, she noticed a major improvement in alertness. Her reaction time on customer calls became faster, and she no longer relied on caffeine to stay sharp in the afternoon. This simple habit—using movement instead of stimulants—allowed her to stay engaged without the energy crashes that often accompany excessive coffee consumption.

The key takeaway? The brain responds quickly to movement. When focus dips, a short burst of physical effort can immediately restore mental clarity.

Relieving Tension for Mental Focus

While intense activity wakes up the brain, gentle stretching helps release built-up tension that can interfere with focus. Hours of sitting —especially in front of screens—cause muscles to tighten, particularly in the neck, shoulders, and lower back. This tension leads to discomfort, which can subtly distract the mind.

Simple stretches, such as neck rolls, spinal twists, or arm reaches, can reset posture and relieve tightness. More importantly, they allow the mind to reset by shifting attention away from mental clutter and back to the present moment.

In 2017, a professional dancer named Aisha Thomas noticed a pattern in her rehearsals—on days when she skipped her warm-up stretches, she found it harder to stay focused while learning new choreography. Frustrated, she decided to test a simple habit: a midday stretch break, even when she wasn't dancing. Every afternoon, she would step away from her computer and spend two minutes stretching her arms, shoulders, and spine. The result? Her ability to retain new information improved, and she felt more mentally present in meetings. The same concept applies beyond dance—stretching doesn't just relieve physical tension; it clears the mind.

For those who work at desks, integrating simple movements into the workday—such as standing up every hour, rolling the shoulders, or twisting the spine—can prevent the buildup of physical discomfort that leads to mental distractions.

Walking as a Focus Booster

Walking isn't just exercise; it's one of the most effective ways to stimulate creativity and problem-solving. Research from Stanford University found that walking can increase creative output by up to 60%. The reason? Rhythmic movement, fresh air, and a change in scenery activate brain pathways associated with divergent thinking—the ability to generate new ideas.

Writers, entrepreneurs, and artists throughout history have relied on walking to unlock breakthroughs. Charles Dickens walked miles every evening to clear his mind, and Steve Jobs famously held walking meetings to encourage creative discussions.

In 2014, a novelist struggling with writer's block tested an experiment—each time he hit a creative wall, he would take a 10-

minute walk around the block. At first, the habit felt insignificant. But after several weeks, he realized that nearly every time he went for a walk, a new idea would emerge. His afternoon walks became a critical part of his creative process, allowing him to finish his novel on schedule.

The lesson? Sitting and thinking harder isn't always the best way to regain focus. Sometimes, stepping away—especially into nature—allows the mind to make connections that weren't visible before.

Movement as a Focus Strategy

The mind doesn't function well in a static environment. A combination of high-energy bursts, gentle stretching, and strategic walking creates a powerful system for sustaining focus throughout the day.

- Use quick bursts of movement to regain alertness within seconds.
- Stretch to relieve tension and reset the mind for deeper concentration.
- Take short walks to enhance creativity and problem-solving.

When integrated into a daily routine, movement becomes a secret weapon for cognitive performance. The best part? It requires no equipment, no extra time, and no complex strategy—just a willingness to get up and move.

Sleep Charge

No matter how optimized your workspace is, how refined your habits are, or how much caffeine you consume, nothing can compensate for a lack of quality sleep. The brain relies on deep rest to consolidate memory, regulate mood, and sustain attention throughout the day.

Yet in a culture that glorifies hustle, sleep is often the first thing sacrificed in the name of productivity.

Ironically, cutting sleep is one of the worst things you can do if you're trying to improve focus. Research has shown that even mild sleep deprivation—losing just one to two hours per night—can lead to cognitive impairment equivalent to having a blood alcohol level of 0.05%. Chronic sleep debt doesn't just make you tired; it fragments attention, slows reaction time, and increases susceptibility to distractions.

The good news? Reclaiming sleep doesn't require drastic lifestyle changes. A few simple shifts in sleep quality, napping strategies, and light exposure can make a profound difference in mental clarity and sustained focus.

REM Boost

REM sleep—the stage of sleep responsible for dreaming—is one of the most critical phases for cognitive function. It plays a crucial role in memory consolidation, emotional processing, and creative problem-solving. But reaching deep, high-quality REM sleep requires more than just spending eight hours in bed.

One of the biggest disruptors of REM sleep is irregular sleep cycles. The body operates on a 90-minute rhythm, known as the ultradian cycle, which also governs sleep stages. When people wake up in the middle of a cycle, they feel groggy and disoriented, a phenomenon known as sleep inertia. By contrast, waking up at the end of a 90-minute cycle leaves you feeling refreshed and mentally sharp.

A well-rested pilot understands this better than anyone. In 2018, a commercial airline captain, Chris Lutterman, struggled with fatigue on long-haul flights. Instead of relying on caffeine or energy drinks, he fine-tuned his sleep schedule, ensuring that even short naps aligned with his body's natural cycles. By timing his rest in 90-minute increments, he maximized deep sleep efficiency, waking up feeling alert rather than sluggish. Over time, this small adjustment dramatically improved his reaction time and mental clarity in high-pressure situations.

Optimizing REM sleep doesn't require sleeping longer—it requires sleeping smarter. Consistent sleep schedules, blackout environments, and proper temperature control (65°F or 18°C is ideal for deep sleep) can make the difference between waking up groggy and feeling fully recharged. The secret is to sleep blind, deaf and cold.

Nap Power

Napping is often viewed as a luxury or a sign of laziness, but science tells a different story. Short, strategic naps have been shown to increase focus, improve mood, and boost cognitive function—often more effectively than caffeine. The key lies in timing.

A 20-minute nap is often referred to as the "power nap" because it provides a significant mental recharge without causing sleep inertia. A study conducted by NASA found that pilots who took a 20-minute nap experienced a 34% improvement in reaction time and a 200% increase in alertness.

The ideal time for napping? Around 2 PM, when the body naturally experiences an energy dip due to circadian rhythms. A student at Harvard University put this theory to the test in 2019. Facing back-to-back lectures and long nights of studying, he struggled with mental fatigue by mid-afternoon. Instead of pushing through the exhaustion, he started taking a 20-minute nap before tackling his most challenging coursework. The difference was immediate—his ability to retain information improved, and his focus lasted longer into the evening.

However, not all naps are created equal. Longer naps that extend beyond 30 minutes risk pulling the body into deep sleep, which can result in grogginess upon waking. The best approach? Keep it short and nap in a quiet, dark environment free from interruptions.

For those who struggle with mid-afternoon slumps, swapping out an extra cup of coffee for a short nap can yield far better results—without the jitters or crash.

Controlling Sleep's Biggest Disruptor

One of the most overlooked aspects of sleep quality is light exposure. The body's sleep-wake cycle is regulated by light, with blue light from screens being the biggest culprit in disrupting natural melatonin production.

In the digital age, exposure to blue light is nearly unavoidable. Phones, computers, and televisions emit wavelengths that signal to the brain that it's still daytime, delaying the body's ability to wind down for rest.

A professional gamer, who regularly competed in late-night tournaments, faced this exact challenge. After experiencing persistent sleep issues and declining reaction times, he adjusted his pre-sleep routine. By setting a strict no-screen rule after 9 PM, using red light filters on his devices, and replacing bedtime screen time with reading, he noticed a dramatic improvement in sleep quality. The result? Faster reflexes, better mental endurance, and higher performance in competitions.

The fix for disrupted sleep due to blue light is simple—eliminate screen exposure at least an hour before bed. If screen use is unavoidable, switching to warmer, red-toned light or wearing blue light-blocking glasses can mitigate some of the effects.

Beyond screens, controlling light in the bedroom can also enhance sleep. Blackout curtains, removing unnecessary light sources, and avoiding sudden light exposure in the middle of the night can improve the body's ability to stay in deep sleep cycles.

Maximizing Sleep for Peak Focus

If there's one non-negotiable element of focus, it's sleep. A well-rested mind is sharper, more resilient to distractions, and capable of deep, sustained work.

- **Prioritize REM sleep** by maintaining a consistent schedule, keeping a cool sleep environment, and aligning rest with 90-minute cycles.
- **Use short naps** as a tool to recharge, ideally around 2 PM, keeping them under 30 minutes to avoid grogginess.
- **Minimize blue light exposure** before bed and create a dark, screen-free environment for deeper sleep.

The body and brain are designed to perform best when well-rested. By making small adjustments to sleep habits, focus becomes easier, memory improves, and energy levels remain steady throughout the day. Sleep isn't just rest—it's the foundation of high performance.

Chapter 9

Focus in the Storm

Some of the world's highest performers—firefighters, emergency room surgeons, pilots—don't get the luxury of a distraction-free environment. They work in chaos, yet their focus remains razor-sharp. What makes the difference? It's not just training or experience. It's their ability to regulate stress, reframe pressure, and create control in the middle of unpredictability.

Distractions are one thing; overwhelming pressure is another. Research shows that high anxiety reduces working memory and impairs decision-making, turning small setbacks into mental roadblocks. But stress itself isn't the enemy—it's how we respond to it.

Stress Flip

Stress is often seen as the enemy of concentration, but in reality, it's a tool—one that can either derail you or sharpen your focus, depending on how you use it. The key lies in shifting perception. Instead of seeing stress as something to escape, high performers use it as fuel.

In high-stakes environments—whether it's a surgeon in the operating room, an athlete in the final seconds of a game, or a firefighter making split-second decisions—stress is unavoidable. But those who excel don't eliminate it. They control their response. By regulating their breath, reframing urgency as a challenge, and anchoring themselves in small, immediate actions, they channel stress into precision rather than panic.

Pressure doesn't have to scatter your focus. When you flip your mindset, it can sharpen it instead.

The Fastest Reset Button

When stress rises, the first thing that changes is breathing. It speeds up, becomes shallow, and sends danger signals to the brain. This triggers a cascade of reactions—higher cortisol, increased heart rate, and fragmented attention. But if you can control your breath, you can reverse that entire response.

We've already covered the **4-7-8 breathing method** in an earlier chapter—where you inhale for four seconds, hold for seven, and exhale for eight. This technique forces the nervous system into a relaxed state, slowing the heart rate and reducing cortisol. It's a method used by military personnel, athletes, and high-pressure professionals to regain control.

Another tool we previously explored, **box breathing**, is widely used by Navy SEALs and first responders. By inhaling, holding, exhaling, and pausing for equal counts, it creates a rhythmic balance that steadies the nervous system. In high-stress environments, this technique is a lifeline—keeping the mind locked in, rather than spiraling out.

Dr. Richard Carmona, former U.S. Surgeon General and a seasoned trauma surgeon, has spoken about how controlled breathing is a non-negotiable skill in the operating room. Before making critical incisions, he would take a deliberate deep breath, hold, and exhale slowly. This simple habit kept his hands steady and his mind sharp, ensuring that stress never dictated his performance.

Breath control doesn't eliminate high-pressure moments—it however ensures that you stay in command of them.

Turning Stress into Focus

Most people view stress as something to avoid. High performers see it as something to use. The difference isn't in the circumstances—it's in the mindset.

Deadlines, constraints, and urgency often sharpen focus rather than dull it. A study from the University of Chicago found that when athletes and professionals are under pressure, their performance improves—provided they see the pressure as a challenge rather than a threat. The key isn't to avoid stress, but reinterpreting it.

Michelin-starred chef Dominique Crenn thrives in the heat of a fully booked dinner service. Her kitchen moves at an unrelenting pace—orders flood in, the grill blazes, and the timing of every dish is critical. Yet, instead of being overwhelmed, she channels the intensity. The stress sharpens her focus. Every movement is intentional, every decision precise.

The same principle applies beyond the kitchen. A well-set deadline can act as a cognitive accelerator rather than a stressor. A physical challenge—like lifting slightly heavier weights—can enhance mental sharpness. Tight constraints can encourage deeper engagement.

The turning point is perception. When stress is framed as fuel rather than friction, it transforms from a blocker into a booster.

. . .

Reclaiming Control in Chaos

When overwhelmed, the natural tendency is to freeze. The to-do list feels endless. The pressure to keep up becomes suffocating. But high performers don't focus on finishing everything—they focus on finishing something.

One overwhelmed parent, juggling work deadlines and a restless toddler, found herself on the verge of burnout. Every task felt impossible to complete. But instead of trying to tackle everything, she focused on micro-wins—responding to one urgent email, preparing a single meal, giving her child five minutes of undivided attention. The momentum of completing one task, then another, helped restore a sense of control.

When stress spikes, three simple principles restore focus:

1. Control the breath. If the body is calm, the mind follows.
2. Reframe the pressure. Stress isn't an enemy if you use it strategically.
3. Stack small wins. Progress—even in tiny doses—prevents paralysis.

No one avoids chaos entirely. But those who master focus learn how to stand steady in the middle of the storm.

Adapt Kit

The ability to focus is often framed as an exercise in discipline—setting rules, creating structure, and eliminating distractions. But in reality, the most productive individuals aren't just disciplined; they're adaptable. They know how to stay focused when things go wrong.

Because things *will* go wrong.

Your perfectly planned work session might be interrupted by an unexpected meeting. Your laptop might freeze in the middle of a crucial deadline. A last-minute request might force you to scrap everything and start over. These are not rare occurrences; they're part of life. But while most people let disruptions derail them, those who truly master focus have a system for staying on track, no matter what.

That's what the Adapt Kit is about—recovering fast when your environment, schedule, or mental state suddenly shifts.

Pivot Signs

Not all disruptions hit like an earthquake. Some creep in slowly, and before you know it, you've wasted an hour spinning your wheels, trying to push forward when what you really need is a shift in approach. The key to staying focused is recognizing when you need to pivot *before* you lose momentum.

The first step is spotting *chaos cues*—subtle signs that your current plan isn't working. Maybe your brain feels foggy, or you keep rereading the same paragraph without absorbing it. Maybe you're facing unexpected resistance, like technical difficulties, or your mind is stuck in a loop of frustration. These signals aren't a reason to quit; they're a sign that you need to adjust.

A powerful way to do this is a quick *plan check*—instead of plowing forward blindly, pause for 30 seconds and ask: *What's the real problem?* Is it an external disruption, like a noisy environment? A mental block, like overcomplicating the task? A workflow issue, like using the wrong tool for the job? Once you pinpoint the issue, tweaking your approach—whether that means moving to a quieter space, switching tasks, or simplifying your process—can save you hours of wasted effort.

In high-pressure environments, being flexible isn't a weakness; it's an advantage. Netflix, for example, started as a DVD rental service. When they noticed streaming technology advancing, they pivoted—despite skepticism. That decision transformed them from a niche company into a global entertainment giant. The same principle applies to focus: if you recognize when your approach isn't working and adjust quickly, you stay ahead instead of falling behind.

Plan B Stash

Disruptions don't just throw off your schedule—they can leave you feeling unmoored, unsure of what to do next. That's why the most effective individuals always have a *Plan B Stash*—pre-set backups that allow them to continue working even when their first option falls apart.

One of the most effective strategies is having a backup workspace. If your usual environment is compromised—say, your home office is too noisy, or your favorite café is crowded—where else can you go? Many top professionals have a secondary work spot ready to go, whether it's a different part of the house, a nearby library, or even an outdoor space.

If technology is your weak link, a tool swap can be a lifesaver. Many writers, for instance, keep a notebook on hand in case their laptop crashes. Similarly, professionals who rely on digital calendars might keep a small planner or sticky notes for emergency scheduling. It's not about ditching technology—it's about having a safety net so that no single failure can halt your work entirely.

Time shifting is another powerful tactic. If your scheduled deep-work session gets interrupted, instead of forcing yourself to work at a suboptimal time, shift the session. Some of the most productive people intentionally leave "buffer blocks" in their day, allowing them to move tasks around without disrupting their entire schedule.

A powerful example comes from bestselling author Stephen King. During a power outage that shut down his workspace, he didn't wait for the lights to come back on—he moved to his garage, used a legal pad, and wrote by flashlight. That adaptability allowed him to keep momentum rather than waiting for the perfect conditions to return.

How to Reboot Focus After an Interruption

Even with backup plans, some distractions will be unavoidable. Meetings run late. Kids need attention. A single email turns into a chain of unexpected work. In those moments, the difference between losing an entire day and regaining focus in minutes comes down to one thing: *the ability to bounce back fast.*

One of the simplest and most effective bounce drills is the *interrupt test.* If you've been pulled away from your work, don't dive back in without checking your focus. Ask yourself: *Am I still engaged with this task, or am I distracted by what just happened?* If your mind is scattered, take a deliberate 1-minute reset before resuming—deep breathing, stretching, or even stepping away for a moment can clear mental residue and allow you to start fresh.

Another technique is using a cue word—a single word or phrase that signals to your brain that it's time to re-engage. Some professionals use "Now," while others prefer something more personal like "Game on" or "Let's go." This seemingly small trick taps into the brain's associative power, helping you transition back into focus mode.

The most effective bounce-back technique is starting small. If a long distraction has thrown you off, don't try to immediately jump back into intense deep work—start with something manageable. This could be rereading the last paragraph you wrote, reviewing your notes, or doing a tiny, low-resistance task to build momentum. The key is to *re-enter work mode gradually* rather than expecting yourself to switch instantly from chaos to deep focus.

A great example of this comes from renowned educator Dr. Maryanne Wolf, who studies attention spans in children. She found that when students are pulled out of deep work, they struggle to re-engage unless given a brief transition activity—like summarizing what they just read or discussing a key point. The same principle applies to adults: *small transitions make big focus recoveries easier.*

Mastering Focus Through Adaptability

Most people think of focus as something fragile—something that can be destroyed by a single distraction. But in reality, the people who are most productive aren't the ones who avoid distractions entirely. They're the ones who know *how to recover quickly.*

The world is unpredictable. Technology fails. People interrupt. Plans change. But none of that has to stop you—because with the right mindset and strategies, you can train your brain to stay locked in, no matter what gets thrown your way.

Rebound Play

Even the best systems for deep work and sustained concentration can collapse if you don't manage your energy. Focus isn't just about eliminating distractions—it's about knowing when to push forward and when to pull back.

Burnout, fatigue, and mental fog don't arrive overnight. They creep in subtly, clouding judgment, slowing output, and making even simple tasks feel exhausting. The problem is that most people only recognize the signs when it's too late—when they're already stuck in a cycle of low productivity, frustration, and exhaustion.

Rebounding quickly isn't just about working harder; it's about listening to the warning signs early and having strategies in place to recharge before focus is lost entirely.

Burnout Flags: Recognizing the Early Signs of Mental Fatigue

Most people don't notice burnout until they've already hit a wall. They keep pushing, ignoring the subtle shifts in their focus and mood, believing that if they just try harder, they'll power through. But the brain doesn't work that way.

Burnout doesn't always look like total collapse. It often begins with *mental fog*—a sense that thoughts are moving slower than usual, that clarity is slipping. Then comes the *grump test*: small annoyances feel bigger, patience wears thin, and frustration creeps in at the slightest disruption.

The next sign is the *slow drop*—output decreases, but not because of lack of effort. Tasks take longer, and the same amount of work that once felt manageable now feels overwhelming. Sleep patterns also shift—whether it's difficulty falling asleep, waking up feeling unrested, or tossing and turning through the night.

Ignoring these signs leads to deeper exhaustion, making it even harder to regain focus. The key is catching burnout before it spirals.

In 2018, Arianna Huffington, founder of *The Huffington Post*, collapsed from exhaustion in her office, hitting her head on her desk. She later described how she had ignored every warning sign—poor sleep, constant fatigue, and declining focus—until her body forced her to stop. That moment led her to reassess her relationship with work and launch *Thrive Global*, a company dedicated to preventing burnout in high-performance professionals.

Most people don't reach that extreme, but they don't have to. Recognizing the early signals and adjusting before burnout takes hold can mean the difference between weeks of struggle and a quick, strategic reset.

Recharge Rites: Practical Ways to Reboot Focus

When energy dips, most people turn to artificial fixes—more caffeine, more hours at the desk, more willpower. But true recovery doesn't come from pushing harder; it comes from resetting the brain in ways that restore clarity without draining more energy.

One of the simplest recharge techniques is the 10-minute reset—stepping away from work without guilt. Studies show that even short breaks can restore cognitive function, provided they are *true* breaks—no scrolling, no checking emails, no half-working. A simple walk, sitting in silence, or closing your eyes for a moment can refresh mental stamina.

Nature is another powerful reset button. Research from the University of Michigan found that even a short walk in a green space can improve focus by up to 20%. Even if a full nature break isn't possible, simply looking at plants, stepping outside for fresh air, or listening to nature sounds can trigger the same effect.

Laughter is another underrated recharge tool. Neuroscientist Sophie Scott has found that laughter reduces cortisol and increases dopamine, making it one of the fastest ways to break mental fatigue. In high-stress environments, quick exposure to humor—whether it's a funny video, a joke, or a conversation with a friend—can instantly shift the brain into a more relaxed, focused state.

Sleep, of course, plays a major role in focus recovery, but when a full night's rest isn't an option, strategic naps can work wonders. A 20-minute power nap has been shown to boost alertness and productivity by up to 200%.

One striking example of this comes from Albert Einstein, who used micro-naps to sustain his deep-thinking sessions. He would sit in a chair holding a spoon over a metal plate; as soon as he dozed off and the spoon dropped, the noise would wake him—allowing him to rest just enough without falling into deep sleep. While most people don't need such an extreme technique, the core principle remains: short, intentional rest can reset the mind without derailing momentum.

Guilt Cleanse: Overcoming the Fear of Taking Breaks

For high-achievers, one of the biggest obstacles to recovery isn't a lack of time—it's guilt. Many people see taking breaks as a sign of weakness or wasted time, believing that pushing through exhaustion is the only way to succeed. But the research is clear: strategic breaks don't reduce productivity—they enhance it.

The key shift is reframing rest as *fuel*, not failure. The world's top performers don't work nonstop—they work in cycles, alternating between intense focus and intentional recovery. Olympians structure their training around periods of rest. Writers step away from their manuscripts to let ideas settle. Entrepreneurs like Elon Musk and Bill Gates schedule "think weeks", where they unplug entirely to regain clarity.

Self-talk plays a critical role in this shift. Instead of thinking, *I'm wasting time by taking a break*, reframe it: *I'm recharging so I can perform at my best*. Studies in cognitive psychology show that the way we talk to ourselves affects our actual cognitive performance. A simple mindset shift—from seeing breaks as indulgent to seeing them as essential—can make a massive difference.

Sometimes, true recovery requires stepping back completely. When painter Henri Matisse was struggling creatively, he took an entire month off from painting. Instead of forcing himself to work through the block, he traveled, explored other art forms, and allowed his mind to wander. When he returned to the canvas, his creativity had been reignited.

The idea of completely stopping work for a period may seem impossible in modern hustle culture. But for those who want to sustain long-term focus, *knowing when to pause is just as important as knowing when to push forward.*

The Art of Sustainable Focus

Focus isn't about forcing the brain into constant high performance. It's about learning how to recognize fatigue early, reset quickly, and recharge without guilt.

Burnout doesn't have to be inevitable. If you can recognize the warning signs—mental fog, declining output, frustration—you can take action before focus is lost entirely. If you build in small but effective recovery strategies—whether it's stepping outside, laughing, or taking a micro-nap—you can sustain clarity without crashing. And if you can shift your mindset to see rest as an essential part of peak performance, you'll never have to choose between working hard and staying sharp.

High performers don't just know how to focus—they know how to recover. And in a world that demands constant attention, that ability is what separates those who thrive from those who burn out.

Chapter 10

The Focus Payoff

Picasso didn't juggle masterpieces—so why should you?

When people think of peak performers—whether artists, inventors, or entrepreneurs—they often picture them as multi-tasking geniuses, handling countless projects at once. But in reality, the best creators and innovators don't spread themselves thin; they go deep.

Pablo Picasso, despite producing an estimated 50,000 works in his lifetime, never worked on multiple masterpieces at once. He immersed himself in one project, finishing it before moving on. Steve Jobs didn't launch dozens of products at Apple—he focused on a handful of revolutionary designs that changed industries. Warren Buffett has often said that saying no to 99% of opportunities is the key to success.

Mastering focus isn't just about eliminating distractions. It's about ensuring that your time and energy go toward the right things. When you learn to direct your attention toward what truly matters, the results don't just show up in your work—they transform your entire life.

Big Wins

The ability to focus isn't just about getting more done—it's about getting the right things done. Many people spend years reacting to whatever demands their attention instead of deliberately choosing what matters most. When you sharpen your focus, you gain more than just productivity. You gain clarity, purpose, and the ability to leave behind a lasting impact.

Focusing deeply on meaningful work is what separates those who create something enduring from those who remain stuck in cycles of distraction. Whether it's an invention that shapes the future, a legacy that outlives you, or simply a body of work that you take pride in, the biggest rewards in life come from sustained focus.

But here's the truth: not all effort leads to meaningful progress. It's easy to waste energy on tasks that feel important but don't actually move you forward. The real power of focus lies in learning to separate what deserves your full attention from what simply fills up your day.

Defining Your Most Important Work

One of the greatest challenges of modern life isn't a lack of ambition—it's too many competing goals. With unlimited opportunities, responsibilities, and distractions pulling at your time, it's easy to fall into the trap of spreading yourself too thin. The key to real progress is ruthless prioritization.

The first step is to identify your top three goals—the things that, if accomplished, would make the biggest difference in your life or work.

This isn't about minor tasks or quick wins; it's about long-term priorities. Everything else is secondary.

When inventor James Dyson set out to revolutionize vacuum cleaners, he wasn't chasing a dozen different projects at once. He dedicated himself entirely to one mission: building a better vacuum. It took 5,127 prototypes and over five years of focused work before he succeeded, but that deep commitment resulted in a product that changed the industry. Dyson's journey proves that the path to mastery isn't about doing more—it's about choosing the right thing and sticking with it.

Once you know your top priorities, the next step is shifting your perspective from short-term tasks to long-term progress. It's easy to get lost in daily to-do lists, but meaningful work happens over weeks, months, and years. Tracking your progress over longer time frames forces you to think beyond immediate deadlines and focus on the bigger picture.

This also means cutting out low-value tasks—the things that feel productive but don't actually contribute to your top three goals. Social media scrolling, unnecessary meetings, busywork that could be automated or delegated—all of these drain your time without moving you closer to success. By removing distractions and streamlining your efforts, you free up mental space for deep, impactful work.

Creating Work That Lasts

In a world that moves fast, most things are designed to be temporary. Trends rise and fall, viral moments fade, and much of what people work on today will be forgotten tomorrow. But true impact comes from work that stands the test of time.

Focusing on depth over volume is what leads to lasting achievements. Many people feel pressured to produce more—more projects, more output, more hustle. But the most influential creators, thinkers, and innovators don't scatter their attention across dozens of projects. They concentrate deeply on fewer things and do them exceptionally well.

Think of Frank Lloyd Wright, one of the most celebrated architects in history. His designs weren't rushed. He took time to craft buildings that would endure for generations, prioritizing quality over speed. One of his most famous works, Fallingwater, was designed with such meticulous attention to detail that it remains an architectural marvel nearly a century later.

This principle applies to any field. Writers, artists, entrepreneurs, and scientists who make a lasting impact do so by investing years—sometimes decades—into perfecting their craft. They resist the temptation to chase trends or rush to the next project and instead focus on creating something truly great.

Focusing on legacy also means recognizing that time is your greatest asset. Every hour spent on distractions is time taken away from meaningful work. Prioritizing focus isn't just about productivity—it's about reclaiming your time for things that actually matter.

One builder, Peter Zumthor, became known for his ability to create timeless structures by resisting the pressure to rush. He worked on projects for years, often turning down lucrative opportunities in favor of doing work he believed in. The result? His buildings are considered some of the finest in modern architecture. By focusing on depth instead of speed, he created a legacy that will outlast him.

Aligning Focus with What Fuels You

Focus is much easier to sustain when it's aligned with something you genuinely care about. Passion isn't just a buzzword—it's a psychological advantage that makes deep work effortless. When you're engaged in something meaningful, distractions lose their grip, time speeds up, and you enter a state of flow.

One way to recognize passion-driven focus is to test the **joy factor**. If you find yourself naturally returning to a particular type of work, thinking about it even when you're not "on the clock," or losing track of time while doing it, those are strong indicators that it's worth prioritizing.

A musician like John Coltrane didn't just play the saxophone—he obsessed over it. He practiced relentlessly, refining his technique for years, not because he had to, but because he was deeply invested in his craft. His focus produced some of the most influential jazz music of all time.

Aligning focus with passion doesn't mean avoiding hard work. Even meaningful work has moments of difficulty and frustration. But passion acts as fuel, making the challenges worth pushing through.

Another approach is to play to your strengths. People achieve greater levels of focus when they work in areas where they naturally excel. If a task feels like an uphill battle every single time, it may not be the right focus. Redirecting energy toward work that aligns with your skills leads to higher levels of achievement.

Finally, understanding the purpose behind your work is essential. When people lose focus, it's often because they've lost sight of why their work matters. Reconnecting with the deeper reason behind what you're doing provides clarity and motivation.

The Ultimate Payoff

The true reward of focus isn't just productivity—it's mastery. It's knowing that your energy is being spent on something meaningful rather than scattered across a hundred minor tasks. Whether it's achieving a lifelong goal, building something that lasts, or simply finding joy in work, focus is the foundation for all of it.

When distractions are stripped away, and your time is spent deliberately, the quality of your work—and your life—transforms. The greatest minds in history weren't superhuman; they were simply masters of attention. And now, with the right habits in place, so can you.

Life Lift

Focus isn't just about deep work or productivity—it's about being fully present in the moments that matter. The same attention that fuels professional success can also transform relationships, deepen connections, and improve overall well-being. Too often, people go through life half-present, splitting their attention between conversations, notifications, and endless mental clutter.

But the ability to focus is the ability to **be here right now**—to listen without distraction, to engage fully, and to experience life without the haze of multitasking. Whether it's quality time with loved ones, strengthening personal boundaries, or fostering better teamwork, focus extends beyond work and into the fabric of everyday life.

The Art of Undivided Attention

In an age of digital overload, one of the rarest gifts you can give someone is your full attention. Conversations are often interrupted by buzzing phones, half-listening responses, and the urge to check notifications. But when you strip away distractions, even ordinary moments become meaningful.

One simple but powerful shift is turning off your phone during key interactions. Studies have shown that even a silent phone on the table reduces the depth of a conversation. When people put their devices away, engagement deepens, conversations become richer, and relationships strengthen.

This principle played out for one couple who found themselves constantly distracted by their phones during dinner. After noticing how often they checked their screens, they committed to a no-tech dinner rule—leaving their phones in another room for the duration of the meal. Within weeks, they noticed a shift: conversations became more engaging, they felt more connected, and their evenings felt longer, as they were no longer fragmented by scrolling or checking messages.

Beyond putting devices away, presence is also about active listening. Simple habits—like maintaining eye contact, resisting the urge to formulate a response while the other person is talking, and asking deeper questions—turn surface-level exchanges into meaningful dialogue.

The ability to be in the moment isn't just beneficial for relationships—it improves memory, emotional well-being, and even decision-making. When you train yourself to focus fully on what's happening now, instead of letting your mind drift to the past or future, you experience life more deeply.

Boundary Gift: Protecting Your Time and Attention

Boundaries aren't just about saying no—they're about protecting what matters most. Without clear limits, your focus will always be at the mercy of other people's demands, last-minute requests, and social expectations.

One of the most overlooked focus drains is the tendency to overcommit—saying yes to too many events, obligations, or favors. Time isn't infinite, and every "yes" to one thing is a "no" to something else. Learning to **guard your time** isn't selfish—it's necessary for deep work, meaningful relationships, and personal well-being.

A parent once struggled with constantly being pulled in different directions—between work, parenting, and social obligations, they had no real time for focused family moments. They decided to implement **"protected hours"**—a two-hour block each evening where they were completely unavailable for work or outside commitments. Phones went away, emails were ignored, and family time became non-negotiable.

The result? A stronger bond with their children, a greater sense of balance, and surprisingly, even higher work efficiency—because without constant context switching, they were able to complete tasks faster during the day.

Beyond personal boundaries, teaching focus to others is just as important. Children, partners, and colleagues all benefit when focus is treated as a shared value. Modeling deep engagement—whether it's reading without distractions, listening without checking messages, or fully committing to a creative project—reinforces that undivided attention isn't just possible; it's essential.

Bringing Focus Into Shared Spaces

Focus isn't just an individual effort—it thrives in environments where attention is respected. Whether at work, in a creative team, or even in a household, shared focus norms create an atmosphere where deep engagement becomes the default.

One of the most effective ways to enhance group focus is through structured collaboration—setting clear expectations around when to engage and when to work independently. Teams that work in flow states together achieve higher-quality results than those constantly interrupted by meetings and messages.

This principle is evident in high-performing creative teams, like those in the music industry. A jazz band, for example, thrives not by playing over each other, but by listening intently, taking turns, and knowing when to step in and when to step back.

One band, facing a creative block while recording an album, decided to eliminate all distractions during rehearsals—no phones, no unnecessary side conversations, just full immersion in the music. The result? They completed their album in record time, with a level of cohesion that only comes from deep, focused collaboration.

Another key element of team focus is reducing unnecessary noise. Many workspaces are built around constant interruptions—open offices, excessive meetings, and always-on communication tools. But research consistently shows that fewer interruptions lead to better performance and deeper thinking.

Companies that implement "focus-friendly" norms, such as setting meeting-free work hours or using asynchronous communication, see significant boosts in productivity and job satisfaction. The key is recognizing that focus isn't about isolation—it's about creating the right balance between deep work and meaningful collaboration.

The Lasting Impact of a Focused Life

Bringing focus into personal life is about presence, balance, and purpose. When attention is divided, life moves faster but feels less fulfilling. When attention is concentrated, even simple moments can be magical.

Being truly present with loved ones, setting clear boundaries, and fostering focused teamwork are all extensions of the same principle: attention is a limited resource, and where you invest it shapes your reality.

Focus isn't just about what you produce—it's about how you experience life. And the more you protect it, the more rewarding life becomes.

Forever Edge

Focus isn't just a skill—it's a way of life. It determines the quality of work produced, the depth of relationships nurtured, and the clarity with which goals are pursued. But lasting focus doesn't happen overnight. It's built through habits, growth, and vision, shaping how attention is used day after day.

The ability to focus deeply isn't just about working harder; it's about creating a structure that reinforces focus naturally. Whether through habit formation, continuous learning, or long-term vision planning, the way attention is managed today determines the outcomes of tomorrow.

Making Focus Automatic

Deep focus isn't something to fight for every day—it should be something that happens on autopilot. The easiest way to do this is through habit stacking—attaching focused work to an existing daily routine.

For example, if coffee is part of the morning routine, pairing it with a dedicated deep work session signals the brain that focus follows caffeine. Over time, this association becomes automatic, reducing the need for motivation.

This principle of habit stacking is used by top performers in various fields. Olympic runner Eliud Kipchoge, known for his record-breaking marathon performances, follows a strict sequence before every training session—tying his shoelaces in the same way, taking a deep breath, and visualizing the run ahead. This routine signals his mind that it's time for complete concentration, making deep focus a natural state rather than a forced effort.

Beyond stacking habits, setting physical cues is another effective strategy. A well-organized workspace that is only used for deep work creates a mental shortcut—the moment someone sits down, their brain associates the location with focus.

Lastly, reinforcement is key. The reward loop—where small wins are acknowledged—ensures habits stick. Whether it's checking off a task list, tracking hours of deep work, or simply reflecting on progress, celebrating consistency helps build the foundation for lifelong focus.

The Relationship Between Focus and Mastery

Mastery in any field isn't just about talent—it's about sustained focus over time. The best performers aren't always the most gifted, but often the ones who stick at it for the longest.

One of the biggest barriers to long-term focus is a fear of failure. People often quit too early when faced with difficulty. But if failure is treated as feedback instead of a stopping point, focus can remain intact through challenges.

In 1985, software engineer John Carmack, co-creator of *Doom* and *Quake*, spent years refining his ability to solve complex programming challenges. He was known for locking himself in his workspace for hours, undistracted by emails or social interactions, breaking down each problem into smaller, solvable components. He believed that the ability to focus for long periods was the true differentiator between an average programmer and a great one. This deliberate practice not only helped him revolutionize the gaming industry but also influenced the way modern game engines are built.

This concept of embracing the struggle is seen across fields. Great musicians don't just practice what they're good at; they deliberately work on their weaknesses. The best athletes don't avoid tough drills; they lean into discomfort because they know growth lies there.

The key is to shift from a fixed mindset ("I'm not good at this") to a growth mindset ("I'm getting better at this"). When focus is fueled by improvement rather than immediate results, the ability to sustain deep work dramatically increases.

The Long Game of Focus

Short-term productivity is meaningless without a long-term vision. Many people work hard without a clear direction, pouring focus into tasks without understanding where they lead. True focus isn't just about what is done—it's about why.

A clear vision acts as a compass, guiding daily decisions and keeping distractions in check. This is why successful individuals define their end goals early.

In 2012, retired aerospace engineer John Collins broke the Guinness World Record for the longest paper airplane flight. Instead of randomly experimenting, he approached it with laser focus—studying aerodynamics, testing materials, and refining his technique over four years. His efforts paid off when his carefully designed plane, thrown by professional quarterback Joe Ayoob, set the record with a 226-foot flight. His focus wasn't just about making a better paper airplane—it was about understanding flight itself.

The same principle applies to any field. Whether it's launching a business, becoming an expert in a subject, or mastering a craft, clarity on the long-term outcome makes focus easier to maintain.

One useful exercise for this is reverse engineering success—imagining the ideal future and breaking it down into steps backward until the present moment is reached. This method clarifies exactly what needs to be done today to move closer to the ultimate goal.

The Lasting Power of Focus

A focused life isn't just about getting more done—it's about doing the right things with intention. It's about waking up each day with clarity, knowing where attention should go, and using it to build something meaningful.

By turning focus into a habit, treating challenges as opportunities for growth, and aligning attention with long-term vision, deep work stops being a struggle and starts being second nature.

This isn't about temporary hacks or fleeting motivation—it's about mastering focus as a way of life. The best part? The more focus is cultivated, the more effortless it becomes.

Because when focus is no longer a battle, life itself becomes limitless.

Conclusion: Your Focus Future

The way you focus shapes the way you live. Every task, every moment of deep work, and every decision to resist distraction builds the foundation of who you become. This isn't just about being more productive—it's about designing a life where your attention works for you, not against you.

Think about the journey you've taken through this book. You've uncovered the myths of multitasking, dismantled the distraction web, designed an environment that fuels deep work, and strengthened the mental resilience needed to stay present. You've seen how world-class performers—from Olympic athletes to scientists and artists—use focus as their greatest competitive advantage. Now, the final step is yours to take.

The Power of a Single Step

Transformation doesn't come from reading—it comes from doing. The biggest mistake people make is waiting for the perfect moment to start applying what they've learned. The truth is, focus isn't something you wait for—it's something you build.

Pick one strategy that resonated with you. Maybe it's setting sacred hours for deep work, implementing the 90-minute flow cycle, or simply turning your phone grayscale to reduce distractions. Whatever it is, start now. Small changes create momentum, and momentum turns into mastery.

Your Focus is Your Legacy

Years from now, people won't remember how many emails you answered or how many hours you spent in meetings. They'll remember what you created, what you built, and the impact you left behind. The ability to focus isn't just about work—it's about being fully present in every aspect of life. It's about being there for your loved ones, pursuing your passions without distraction, and making decisions with clarity and confidence.

The modern world rewards busyness, but true success comes from depth. Those who learn to master focus will shape the future—whether in business, creativity, or personal fulfillment. You have the tools. You have the knowledge. Now, you have the choice.

Your Next Move

This isn't the end of the journey—it's the beginning. Focus isn't a skill you master once and forget; it's a muscle you strengthen every day. Some days will be harder than others. Some days, distractions will win. But every time you choose deep work over shallow attention, you're reinforcing a habit that will change everything.

The world is full of noise, but you don't have to be a part of it. You can be the person who creates, who builds, who thrives in the quiet power of deep work.

What will you focus on today?

Keeping the Focus Alive

Now that you have the tools to reclaim your attention, master deep work, and unlock your full potential, it's time to pass that knowledge forward.

By sharing your honest review on Amazon, you'll help other readers—students, entrepreneurs, professionals, and creatives—discover the same strategies that helped you.

Most people struggle with focus, unsure where to begin. Your review could be the push they need to take back control of their time and energy.

Thank you for being part of this movement. Focus is a skill that grows stronger when we share what we've learned—and your voice helps keep it alive.

If this book made a difference for you, I'd be incredibly grateful if you could leave a review. Simply scan the QR code below or visit this link:

[https://www.amazon.com/review/review-your-purchases/?asin=BOOKASIN]

Jordan Cross

References

Baumeister, R. F., & Tierney, J. (2011). *Willpower: Rediscovering the Greatest Human Strength*. Penguin Press.

Cal Newport. (2016). *Deep Work: Rules for Focused Success in a Distracted World*. Grand Central Publishing.

Duhigg, C. (2012). *The Power of Habit: Why We Do What We Do in Life and Business*. Random House.

Goleman, D. (2013). *Focus: The Hidden Driver of Excellence*. Harper.

Kahneman, D. (2011). *Thinking, Fast and Slow*. Farrar, Straus and Giroux.

McGonigal, K. (2012). *The Willpower Instinct: How Self-Control Works, Why It Matters, and What You Can Do to Get More of It*. Avery.

Pinker, S. (1997). *How the Mind Works*. W.W. Norton & Company.

Sapolsky, R. M. (2004). *Why Zebras Don't Get Ulcers: The Acclaimed Guide to Stress, Stress-Related Diseases, and Coping*. Henry Holt & Co.

Schwartz, T. (2010). *The Way We're Working Isn't Working: The Four Forgotten Needs That Energize Great Performance*. Free Press.

Smallwood, J., & Schooler, J. W. (2015). The Science of Mind-Wandering: Empirically Navigating the Stream of Consciousness. *Annual Review of Psychology*, 66(1), 487-518. https://doi.org/10.1146/annurev-psych-010814-015331

Sweller, J. (1988). Cognitive Load During Problem Solving: Effects on Learning. *Cognitive Science*, 12(2), 257-285. https://doi.org/10.1207/s15516709cog1202_4

Trafton, A. (2016). Neuroscientists Identify Brain Mechanisms That Help Suppress Distracting Sensory Information. *MIT News*. https://news.mit.edu/2016/neuroscientists-identify-brain-mechanisms-suppress-distracting-information-1017

Van der Linden, D. (2011). The Urge to Mind-Wander: Understanding the Triggers of Task-Unrelated Thoughts. *Consciousness and Cognition*, 20(2), 472-478. https://doi.org/10.1016/j.concog.2010.10.003

Wang, Y., & Tchernev, J. (2012). The "Facebook Addiction" Factor: The Relationship Between Social Media Use and Psychological Outcomes. *Computers in Human Behavior*, 28(6), 2207-2214. https://doi.org/10.1016/j.chb.2012.06.002

Ward, A. F., Duke, K., Gneezy, A., & Bos, M. W. (2017). Brain Drain: The Mere Presence of One's Own Smartphone Reduces Available Cognitive Capacity. *Journal of the Association for Consumer Research*, 2(2), 140-154. https://doi.org/10.1086/691462

www.ingramcontent.com/pod-product-compliance
Lightning Source LLC
Chambersburg PA
CBHW060613080526
44585CB00013B/808